The Ten Creepiest Places in America

ALLAN ZULLO

Troll

ACKNOWLEDGMENTS

I wish to thank the following researchers, libraries, and organizations for assisting me in putting this book together:

Ardmore (Pennsylvania) Library; Glenn Campbell, Area 51 Research Center; Carla Chadick; *The Islander,* Pensacola Beach, Florida; Dale Kaczmarek, Ghost Research Society; Dawn Lemay, Kelley Library, Salem, New Hampshire; Carol Marcks, East Baton Rouge (Louisiana) Parish Library; Marfa (Texas) Public Library; John McGran; Martha Moffett; and Gwenevere Tucker, Georgetown County (South Carolina) Public Library.

Their cooperation and efforts were greatly appreciated.

*To my good friend Bob Plumb,
with hopes he will climb to new heights both on
and off those challenging rock faces.*

CONTENTS

Introduction 7

GEORGETOWN COUNTY
South Carolina 9

MARFA LIGHTS VIEWING AREA
Marfa, Texas 20

AREA 51
Near Rachel, Nevada 29

THE MYRTLES PLANTATION
St. Francisville, Louisiana 39

AMERICA'S STONEHENGE
North Salem, New Hampshire 49

GENERAL WAYNE INN
Merion, Pennsylvania 55

CHACO CANYON
New Mexico 63

GULF BREEZE
Florida 71

BROWN MOUNTAIN GHOST LIGHTS VIEWING AREA
Brown Mountain, North Carolina 81

HANNAH HOUSE
Indianapolis, Indiana 88

INTRODUCTION

You may know of creepy places that send shivers up your spine—the spooky, empty house that everyone says is haunted . . . the thick, dark woods where gnarled trees creak and groan . . . the deep, mysterious cave you were warned never to enter.

They seem scary because usually they are shrouded in legends designed to give people the chills. But some eerie places are spooky because strange, unexplained things really do happen there.

So where are the creepiest places in America? That question was put to experts in various fields of paranormal phenomena. Based on their opinions, this book features ten places from all parts of the country that are guaranteed to give visitors the creeps.

This book will take you to incredibly haunted real places—including the most ghost-ridden county in America. You'll also travel to some Texas rangeland and a North Carolina mountain where bizarre balls of light dance and dart at night. You'll go to a ruin in New Hampshire that rivals the mystery of Stonehenge. And you'll visit the Florida town where more UFOs are sighted than anywhere else.

Who knows, maybe on your next family vacation you'll encounter one of these creepy places for yourself!

GEORGETOWN COUNTY
South Carolina

Georgetown County, South Carolina—including the tiny seaport that bears its name and nearby Pawleys Island—is considered by many experts the most haunted county in the United States.

Residents and visitors alike have reported ghostly wanderers on the windswept shores and moss-draped estates. In fact, so many ghosts have been seen in the area that the local chamber of commerce sponsors a tour of haunted, centuries-old plantations, townhouses, and graveyards.

"I've studied similar lore around the world, but this area seems to have more ghost legends per square inch than any other place I know," declared local historian Charles Joyner, of the University of South Carolina's Coastal Carolina College.

The pages of Georgetown's history are filled with the kind of emotionally charged events that believers in the paranormal say attract ghosts. The Revolutionary War and Civil War destroyed families and fortunes. Hurricanes and diseases such as diphtheria and malaria ruined lives.

"There has been so much bittersweet history here, so much love, so much sorrow," said Bill Oberst, executive director of the chamber of commerce. "And the area has somehow absorbed it all. You can smell it in the salt air, hear it in the waves, feel it under the trees."

"Most residents accept and even appreciate the ghosts," said Barbara Baxter, who claims her Georgetown home is haunted by the spirit of a British soldier who fought in the Revolutionary War. In fact, when researchers from Duke University wanted to investigate the spirit in her home, Baxter turned them down. "I didn't want them to 'bust' my ghost," she said. "We like him."

Jayne Ware, a parapsychologist from Winston-Salem, North Carolina, has investigated Georgetown's phantoms many times. She said the area is the nation's "hot spot" for roaming spirits.

Here is a sampling of the many ghosts that haunt Georgetown County:

ALICE'S GHOST

Alice Flagg is perhaps the area's most famous ghost. Her story is a simple yet tragic one.

Alice was the daughter of a wealthy family who lived on a magnificent estate called the Hermitage. In 1848, when she was sixteen years old, Alice fell in love with, and secretly became engaged to, a young merchant. But his occupation and position in life put him far below the Flagg family's high social standing.

Because she knew her family would disapprove of the relationship, Alice secretly wore the engagement ring her beloved gave her on a chain around her neck. She soon was sent to school in Charleston, where she became seriously ill. Her older brother Allard sent a carriage to bring Alice back, but by the time she arrived, she was delirious from deadly typhoid fever.

While Alice lay on her bed, Allard discovered the ring dangling from her necklace. In a fit of rage, he ripped it off and threw it into a nearby stream. The sick girl begged for her ring back, but to no avail. She died soon afterward and was buried in All Saints Cemetery.

Since Alice's death, her spirit has been seen many times in the graveyard. She appears as a lovely young woman in the very same elegant ball gown in which she was buried.

Her gravestone rests at the edge of the Flagg family plot. The grave is different from the others in its simplicity. It's a flat marker on the ground and carved with one simple word: "Alice." All the other Flaggs buried in the graveyard have stand-up tombstones with tender words and ornate carvings.

A well-worn path surrounds Alice's grave. This circular track was made by the feet of thousands of visitors—curious tourists, sentimental residents, ghost-hunting teenagers, and the lovelorn. They believe the legend that if you walk thirteen times around the grave backward, Alice will appear.

There are variations on that legend. Some people say you must walk backward around her grave at midnight, or during the full moon. Others claim that instead of seeing her ghost, you will feel a strange tug on your ring.

Alice's grave is usually covered with flowers, pictures, notes, and other small offerings left by those who long for a glimpse of this beautiful restless spirit.

THE GRAY MAN

Another famous ghost in Georgetown County is the dead man who walks the beach at Pawleys Island, warning of a fierce storm or hurricane.

He is known simply as the Gray Man.

Back in 1822, a young man who had been abroad for two years was joyfully returning to the island to see his fiancée. On the way to her house, he and his servant raced their horses. The young man took a shortcut through a marshy area—and straight into tragedy. The horse and rider became caught in quicksand.

The servant, hearing his master's cry for help, tried to save him. But there was no rope or branch long enough to reach the victim. The young man and his horse sank beneath the quicksand and died.

His fiancée was stricken with grief. For days she ambled heartbroken along the beach. One day she saw the figure of a young man dressed in gray. As she walked toward him, her heart began to race. He looked exactly like her beloved. Just as she came within a few yards of him, he disappeared in a sudden swirl of mist.

When she told her family what she had seen, they thought that the shock of her beloved's death was beginning to affect her mind. That night she dreamed she was in a tiny boat tossed in heavy seas as wreckage floated all around her. But soon she saw her love beckoning her toward him on a high sand dune. Then she woke up from her dream.

The dream upset her so much that the next day her family took her to a physician in Charleston sixty miles (96 km) away. Within hours after the family had left, a savage hurricane struck Pawleys Island, sweeping out to sea almost all the houses and most of the island residents.

The girl then realized that her beloved's ghostly appearance on the beach and in her dream ultimately saved her life and the lives of her family. Back then, there was no way to predict when or where a hurricane would strike.

Ever since, many people have seen the Gray Man— always right before a severe storm.

In 1893 the Gray Man appeared to several residents, who then fled the area. Moments later a surprise tidal wave battered the island. Shortly after he was seen by two people on Magnolia Beach, a vicious hurricane killed everyone there except the two who saw him.

During a visit to the island in the early 1950s, a grandmother saw a strange man walking along the water's edge. He was dressed in gray from head to toe. To her shock, he became less and less visible. Within seconds, what had once been a man was just a grayish blur. Then he disappeared. The following day the island was flooded by a harsh storm. The woman and her family escaped unharmed.

In the fall of 1954, Bill Collins, a Georgetown car dealer who lived on Pawleys Island, was on his deck watching the ocean when he spotted the Gray Man.

"As I stood there, I saw someone walking along the beach," Collins later told reporters. "I was curious because there are so few people on the island in October.

"When the person coming toward me got in close focus, he simply vanished. I went down to the beach and searched, but there was no sign of a living soul. What puzzled me was the fact that because of the high dunes, there was no way for anyone to get off the beach without my seeing him. My wife was amazed when I went back and told her about it."

Word soon reached the island that a bad storm was fast approaching. Shortly after Collins and his family left the island, Hurricane Hazel washed away houses and thirty-foot (9-m) dunes. Incredibly, Collins' house was untouched. "Even the TV antenna did not blow down," he said. "That's part of the Gray Man legend—no harm comes to those who see him."

THE GUNN GHOST

Prince Frederick's Episcopal Church outside of town was going to be a place of worship for plantation owners, but it was never finished because of the Civil War. Only the church's ornate tower still stands.

One of the architects of the church was a Scotsman named Gunn. While measuring the roof, he slipped and plummeted to his death, cursing the place as he fell. Over the years, witnesses have reported spotting his ghostly figure walking along a roof that no longer exists. He is carrying a tape and a yardstick. As soon as he is discovered, he disappears with a blood-curdling scream.

At the exact moment the sun sets, phantom music is sometimes heard coming from the uncompleted church. In 1987 parapsychologist Jayne Ware visited the deserted remains of the church. She and a television sound man who was with her claim they heard the haunting music. "It lasted only a few seconds, but it seemed like a full choir," she said.

THE LADY IN WAITING

Before the Civil War, a prominent local family lived in a stately home known as the Heriot-Tarbox house. Their only child was a beautiful daughter who led a sheltered life of tutors, music teachers, and pet dogs.

But then she fell in love with a sailor. When her father found out, he ordered the boat's captain to keep the sailor on the ship whenever it was docked in Georgetown. During the ship's stay, the girl was confined to her room.

But the two young lovers found a way to see each other. She would place a lighted lamp in her window as a signal to meet in her garden after everyone else was asleep. For twenty years the couple met secretly in the garden each time his ship was in port. But for some unknown reason, they never were able to marry each other.

Then one day he stopped coming. As the years passed, the lonely lady continued to light a lamp in her window, hoping in vain that her sailor would return. Eventually she died.

Ever since, people have reported seeing an unexplained light coming from her room. Other passersby say they've seen a dim, fading image of a woman walking with her dogs in the spot where the young girl and her lover used to meet in the garden.

THE STAIRWAY SPIRIT

During the Revolutionary War, the Henning-Miller house was occupied by British troops. One night the alarm sounded, and the soldiers rushed out of the house. A young soldier jumped from his bed and started down the stairway, buttoning his jacket as he went. When he reached an uneven step, he tripped and plunged down the stairs. He broke his neck in the fall and was killed.

Since the tragic accident, many people have tripped on that very same step—but no one has fallen down the stairs. They claim that just as they are about to lose their balance, they experience a strange sensation of suddenly being held and steadied by invisible hands.

Several years ago a woman almost fell on the step, but felt someone catch her. When she looked to see who had helped her, she saw the ghost of a smiling British soldier with a partially unbuttoned jacket.

THE SAD LITTLE BOY

In the early 1800s, a family with only one child, a daughter, lived in the Waterman-Kaminski house. She was lonely, so her cousins from New England often visited her.

The children enjoyed playing together. When the time came for the cousins' family to return north, the youngest child, a boy, begged to remain a little longer. His parents reluctantly agreed to let him stay behind.

Two days after the little boy's family left, their ship sank in a storm off the North Carolina coast, killing all on board. The grief-stricken boy spent much of each day sitting in his room alone, staring blankly out of the window into the garden. When he was ten years old, he died from a high fever.

Soon after the funeral, the family began to hear sad, soft whimpering coming from the boy's room. One afternoon, a maid was putting away linens in the room when she saw the ghost of a crying child in a rocking chair, gazing out the window. He then vanished, but the chair continued to rock.

The dead boy's cousin moved into his room and waited for his spirit to appear. She saw his ghost many times in the rocking chair. But whenever she reached out to comfort him, he disappeared. His chair, however, continued to rock.

Occasionally a passerby claims to have seen the sad face of a little boy staring out of the window of the house.

THE BELL RINGER

Before the Civil War, a dedicated physician named Dr. Tucker owned the sprawling and beautiful Litchfield Plantation. Whenever he was needed, he would hop onto his horse and make house calls, often late into the night.

On such night calls, Dr. Tucker insisted that the gate to the plantation be locked behind him. Upon his return, he would strike a bell next to the gate with the handle of his riding crop. A gatekeeper who lived nearby was responsible for hearing the bell and letting the doctor in.

Sometimes the gatekeeper slipped away at night to visit friends and failed to get back in time. The tired doctor would give up pounding on the bell, tie his horse to the bell post, climb over a split-log fence, and walk down the long avenue of oaks to the house. Then he would use the small private back stairway to his room to avoid disturbing the family.

Years after the doctor's death, the new owners of the Litchfield Plantation claimed they could hear the bell at the gate clanging, as if the doctor wanted to be let in. Whenever the owners went to investigate, they failed to find anyone at the entrance. Finally, they removed the bell. They didn't mind the doctor's ghost paying a visit, but they were tired of the bell waking them up in the middle of the night.

Despite the bell's removal, Dr. Tucker's spirit continues to haunt the plantation. Over the years, the phantom has been spotted on the back stairs. Not only that, but passersby have reported seeing a ghostly form of a man on a horse by the entrance to the estate.

THE GADSDEN GHOST

In the 1700s, South Carolina state assemblyman Christopher Gadsden owned the Beneventum Plantation. A blunt, forceful man, Gadsden encouraged the colonists to rebel against England. He designed one of the most famous of all the colonial flags—the yellow banner with a drawing of a coiled snake bearing thirteen rattles and the words "Don't Tread On Me."

After his death from a fall off a horse, Gadsden's spirit returned to the plantation, where he has been haunting the house ever since.

In 1957 the Fred Lee family bought the old plantation and heard stories of how earlier owners had seen Gadsden's ghost.

"The first thing we became aware of was when we came into the house in the late afternoon. We could hear things, soft sounds like people whispering in church and the distant, faint notes of organ music," recalled Mrs. Lee.

The family assumed their imaginations were working overtime. But then they began to wonder, after talking to an elderly couple who had been caretakers of the plantation for the previous owner. The couple said they often heard strange footsteps and doors slamming when no one was there. They were so scared by the unexplained noises that they refused to enter the house alone.

The Lees took such stories with a grain of salt—until one night they heard their kitchen door open. They were certain they had locked it before going upstairs. Then they heard the clang of a large kitchen spoon as it was dropped into the sink.

Suspecting an intruder, the Lees cautiously went down to investigate. But all was in perfect order. The door was locked, and no metal spoon lay in the sink. Puzzled, they went to bed. Yet night after night they heard the same sounds. The family soon accepted the noise as coming from a "hungry ghost."

One day the Lees' thirteen-year-old daughter Carolyn was dressing upstairs when she had a feeling that someone was staring at her. She turned around and saw the shadowy figure of a tall man clad in black. Carolyn became hysterical and ran downstairs to tell her parents. They found no one in her room nor any way for someone to sneak out without being seen. The family became convinced that she had seen Gadsden's ghost.

The spirit appeared to Carolyn a second time and then to Fred Lee's mother in 1977. Except for the noises and occasional visits, the phantom has never harmed anyone.

THE PARTY CRASHERS

In the early 1800s the Morgan-Ginsler house was built for a wealthy merchant. But Union troops took it over during the Civil War. Sick and wounded soldiers from nearby battles were brought in for treatment. The dining room was used as an operating room, and some soldiers died there.

Following the war, the merchant and his family returned to the house. They found it in good condition, except for a few pieces of damaged furniture.

Several years later the first Georgetown Confederate reunion was held in the home. The party lasted until the early hours of the next morning. After everyone was in bed, the family heard a crash in the dining room. The owner rushed to see what was wrong, but found nothing that could have caused the noise.

Ever since, unexplained loud crashes and thuds have continued to come from that particular room.

PLATEYES

Some residents of the area fear shape-changing ghosts known as "Plateyes."

Ambroze Gonzales, author of many books on the area, wrote that the Plateye, peculiar to the Georgetown coast, is "the weirdest and most fearsome thing" ever to harass people at night. "Plateyes appear to old and young of both sexes, sometimes in the form of a small dog or other animal, while at other times they may float like wraiths along the marshes or [lonely] paths, or stoop like low-hung clouds and envelop the victim."

The ghostly animal will glare at its victim with eyes of fire before lunging at him. Just as the victim expects to be attacked, the Plateye vanishes.

According to Gonzales, some people believe that a person who claims to have encountered a Plateye actually may have fallen asleep while walking. This theory holds that such a person suffered a nightmare in which the Plateye was about to strike. But when the victim awoke, he discovered that the Plateye had gone. Gonzales said believers still dread encounters with Plateyes just as many Europeans feared werewolves not so long ago.

* * *

From Plateyes to lost souls, from Alice to the Gray Man, Georgetown County remains the place to be for encounters with the spirit world.

MARFA LIGHTS VIEWING AREA
Marfa, Texas

For more than one hundred years, bizarre small balls of light have amazed and awed onlookers by flickering, dancing, and darting at night in and around a lonely stretch of rangeland near Marfa, Texas.

As befuddling as they are bedazzling, the strange Marfa Lights are one of North America's great mysteries—because to this day no one knows what they are.

Stories of the Marfa Lights stretch from odd to downright spooky. Some people claim the lights seem to have intelligence, because they act friendly and playful at times. But the lights also have a darker nature, too. They have frightened many residents. And they have chased or followed cars for several miles before vanishing into the night.

The Marfa Lights have been pursued from the air and ground, spotted by tourists and scientists, photographed and even televised. The lights were featured on the hit TV show *Unsolved Mysteries*.

By most accounts they are unexplained points of light no bigger than a basketball, usually white but sometimes colored, that appear in places where lights have no reason to be. Witnesses report that the lights move randomly, rise into the air, change color, or split into multiple lights that veer off at separate angles.

The lights appear when the sky is dark, on or slightly above the horizon. A light will suddenly appear where there was total darkness. It may flicker for a while before dividing into two or more lights. They sometimes glimmer white, green, or blue. At other times they blaze up into yellow or orange. They glow as softly as stars and sometimes shine as brightly as headlights. They can be so intense that they cast shadows on nearby plants.

As many as eleven lights have appeared at one time, moving, bobbing, flickering, and then fading away. Sometimes they stay in the sky for a long while, or disappear as quickly as they came. Most of the time the lights entertain and confound onlookers from far away.

About eight miles (13 km) southeast of Marfa is a stretch of rangeland called Mitchell Flat. In the distance, about thirty miles (48 km) away, stand the rugged Chinati Mountains. It is across Mitchell Flat and up against these mountain walls that the lights bob and blink.

The lights are seen about 125 times a year, during all seasons, at night, usually between eight P.M. and two A.M. The best viewing is on a clear night. However, the lights have been visible on cloudy nights as well.

Jeff Henderson, a reporter for the Lubbock (Texas) *Avalanche-Journal,* said that when he saw the lights for the first time, "the hair on the back of my neck tingled, and a chill went down my spine, yet it was a warm night."

At one time during the sighting, he and his fellow witnesses saw eleven lights shining on the distant horizon. "One of the lights traveled across the darkness a short distance and then went back to its original position," Henderson reported. "Another one moved. Several blinked on and off. The first one rapidly grew larger in size and intensity. The color of the light changed from white to a fiery orange.

"For the most part, an observation of the lights is a nonthreatening experience. There are times, however, when one of the lights seems to be angry, and it grows in size and changes to a reddish-orange in color as if transmitting a warning."

To many people, the lights are creepy because they seem to have a mind of their own.

In 1974 Samuel Whatley was driving home shortly before dawn from his night job as a computer operator when he saw what he thought were car lights speeding toward him on a road east of town. Suddenly a cantaloupe-sized globe of orange-red light appeared and hovered a few feet outside the rolled-down window of his pickup truck.

"I was scared," he admitted later to reporters. "I was crawling out of my skin." He said he floored the accelerator, but the globe stayed with him for about two miles (3 km) before disappearing.

Joe Skelton, of nearby Alpine, Texas, who has seen the lights several times in the area, had a similar experience. Once, he and his wife were driving late at night near Marfa. In the rearview mirror, he noticed what he thought was "an eighteen-wheeler [truck] lit up like a Christmas tree."

Fearing he was about to be run over or blown off the road, Skelton turned to look over his left shoulder. "Nothing," he recalled. "Gone. Just like that."

Geologists J. Pat Kinney and Elwood Wright had several eerie experiences with the lights. The men were surveying uranium deposits around the Chinati Mountains near Marfa in 1969 when they heard townsfolk talking about the mysterious lights. So the men went to Mitchell Flat to investigate.

They made several trips and kept a journal of their sightings. Although they never found out what the lights were, their attempt remains one of the few serious tries by trained personnel to find out the cause of the phenomenon.

One night in 1973, the two geologists were sitting in their

car with the lights out and the motor running near an abandoned air base ten miles (16 km) east of Marfa around ten P.M.

"There were about eight range horses within fifty feet (15 m) of us," Wright recalled. "The horses began whinnying and then they took off, and almost instantaneously two lights—with terrific speed and very low—came right over the horses."

The lights, which appeared to be about half the size of a basketball, moved behind some bushes and hovered briefly a few hundred feet away before vanishing.

"I'll never forget it, I'll guarantee you that," said Kinney. "Those lights are for real. Boy, I mean they were moving. We had the impression they were going 150 to 200 miles (240 to 320 km) an hour."

The men said one of the lights stopped in the middle of the road and hovered about three feet (1 m) off the ground and one hundred feet (30 m) in front of their car. They watched it for about forty-five seconds. Then it brightened, pulled away, and flew east toward the old air base.

"We just sat there, and we both felt so stupid," said Kinney. "It had intelligence, definitely."

Wright said he also came away with a feeling that he had been in the presence of something with intelligence.

"I really and truly don't have any idea what it was," he said. "It kind of looked like it was playing with us. It was a heck of a lot smarter than we were."

The late *Dallas Morning News* columnist Frank X. Tolbert wondered if he was once a victim of the Marfa Lights' playfulness. At first, wrote Tolbert, he mistook the almost searchlight-brilliant dot in the sky for the planet Venus. When it acted strangely, he decided to photograph it. The trouble was that every time Tolbert stopped the car to take a picture, the light winked out.

Mrs. Hallie Stillwell, of nearby Alpine, has seen the lights many times. "They're just weird," she said. "The first time I saw them they scared me to death.

"They usually come out after a rainy spell and on a dark night. They light up and run across the mountain, kind of like a grass fire."

Local county judge Charlie Henderson scoffed at disbelievers. "The people who don't want to believe in the lights say they're car lights. But they're not, I assure you, they're not."

Judge Henderson said he saw distant lights that went in opposite directions and bobbed up and down. Once, he said, he was hunting rabbits on Mitchell Flat when "about midnight, I saw a light shining right down a little canyon I was in. It looked like the headlight on a freight train." Then it vanished.

When Jeanie and Ritchie Reynolds bought their ranch on Mitchell Flat years ago, the real-estate agent asked them if they had ever heard of the Marfa Lights. When they shook their heads, he said, "Well, you're living right on top of them now."

"I was scared to death," Jeanie recalled. "I didn't know if they were ghosts or what."

They still don't know after seeing the lights several times.

The first time they saw one of the lights, she said, "it was a big glowing ball of white that seemed to go away and then come closer. I guess it got within about a mile of the house. It seemed to have a transparent circle around it." They watched the hovering light for about thirty minutes, until it finally faded away.

The first modern-day sightings of the Marfa Lights were reported by Robert Ellison in 1883. Robert, then sixteen, helped move three thousand head of cattle through Paisano

Pass, east of Marfa. He noticed strange starlike flickers against the Chinati Mountains.

He assumed they were Apache campfires burning at the base of the distant mountains. However, when he and his men scoured the area later, they didn't find any signs of the Native Americans.

In fact, the Apaches themselves already had their own legends about the lights. Among their more popular tales: The lights were falling stars dropped to earth; lightning bolts were stored in the rugged mountains by the Great Spirit; the lights belonged to the Apache chieftain Alsate, who was betrayed by the Spanish and was lighting the way home for his fallen warriors.

By the turn of the century, ranchers who had seen the Marfa Lights had their own explanations—from ghosts to gremlins. According to one tale, a rancher was lost in a blinding storm in the Chinati Mountains. He turned from his present course when he saw a floating light. He followed the light, which guided him to the shelter of a cave. When the storm stopped, he emerged from his shelter—and realized that had he not been guided by the light, he would have walked right off the edge of a cliff and down a steep canyon. The light, he claimed, had saved his life.

Some observers said the lights were the lanterns of ghostly members of a wagon train massacred by Native Americans. During both world wars, others claimed the lights were from a secret German army hiding in the mountains.

The most outlandish legend says that in the 1940s, a government scientist was working on a super-secret project— the development of a very dangerous nuclear laser device. During a failed test in a remote laboratory in the Chinati Mountains, the laser-generated light became lost in space and time. The Marfa Lights, according to this tale, are the time-warped laser lights.

During World War II, Mitchell Flat was the site of an air base used to train bomber pilots. Some witnesses at the air base claimed they saw the Marfa Lights line up in a formation mimicking a landing strip to lure unsuspecting pilots and their crews to their deaths. Another account said that the lights were glowing gremlins trying to cause planes to crash against the mountains.

According to Fritz Kahl, who was an instructor at the base and lives in Marfa, the military investigated the Marfa Lights and failed to find a satisfactory explanation.

Pilots tried tracking the lights without success. When men in jeeps reported seeing the lights hovering around the searching airplanes, the plane crews said they saw nothing. When the lights were sighted near the ground by pilots, the men in jeeps saw nothing.

Kahl said that whenever you approach one of the lights, it disappears. "It's like trying to catch a rainbow."

He tried several times to follow the lights in an airplane. Like everyone else who has tried to track down the lights, he didn't have much luck.

"I once flew at night trying to find the lights," he recalled. "I could see them from the plane. It's a low glow from the air—yellow and red. The color varies. They move around.

"They are dull, not focused, a soft yellow to a soft red, to other off-colors. There is some vertical movement, but more horizontal. I never felt hostility from them. As far as I'm concerned, they're kind of friendly."

In the 1960s a rancher hired a helicopter with plans to fly over one of the lights, fix its position, hover over it at low altitude, then land beside it. The plan worked fine—until the rancher and pilot flew directly over the light. Then it flickered out. They landed where it had been and found nothing but grass.

Out on the range, the Marfa Lights continue to bounce, divide, and disappear just as they have for years.

The citizens of this sleepy West Texas ranch town of 2,500, located about two hundred miles (320 km) southeast of El Paso, have mixed feelings about the lights. They are happy that the mysterious lights have put Marfa on the map, attracting people from all over the world.

On the other hand, residents are annoyed by sightseers who rudely trample on private property, hoping to get a better view of the lights. To curb trespassers, the town created an official viewing location, a paved area near the gate of the abandoned airfield, nine miles (14.5 km) east of Marfa along US Highway 67/90. Light-lookers can park and scan the horizon without disturbing the residents of Mitchell Flat.

Besides the legends, the Marfa Lights have produced a bumper crop of at least seventy-five explanations. But every theory yet proposed seems to have flaws. Among the most popular theories, the lights are:

• Jack rabbits hopping around in the dark with glowworms clinging to their fur. But that doesn't explain why most of the sightings are of lights floating in the air.

• Minerals in the mountains that tend to glow in the dark. But no such minerals have been found there.

• St. Elmo's fire, the static electricity known to light up ships' masts or airplane wings. But Mitchell Flat doesn't have any obvious source of such electricity.

• Swamp gas, the vapors caused by rotting vegetation that occasionally burst into flame. But there aren't any swampy areas on the rangeland.

• Ranch lights or car headlights. But these lights appear in areas where there are no homes or roads. Besides, the lights were seen before the invention of electricity.

• Moonlight reflecting off large veins of mica. But the

lights have been seen on cloudy and moonless nights. Besides, there is hardly any mica in the region.

• Mirages. Lights from great distances have been known to be reflected in the atmosphere and focused on a different location. But no one can explain why such an effect would occur so frequently near Marfa.

Until the truth is known—if it ever will be—the Marfa Lights will continue to entertain and bewilder all who watch them.

The residents accept the lights as an eerie fact of life and are in no hurry to solve the mystery. Said Curt Laughlin, the superintendent of nearby McDonald Observatory, "I hope we never find out what the Marfa Lights are. Some things in our lives need to remain mysteries."

Added Harold Surratt, a civil engineer in Alpine, "I've heard the theories, and all of them are easily disputed. The Marfa Lights are a mystery—and frankly I prefer it that way. It's more fun not knowing."

AREA 51

Near Rachel, Nevada

In the high desert of the Nevada outback, far from any town, sits one of the most mysterious locations in the United States—Area 51.

Miles in all directions—along dry lake beds, sagebrush-dotted valleys, and steep mountains—are absolutely off-limits to ordinary civilians. Those foolish enough to set foot in this restricted land risk getting arrested and possibly shot to death.

That's because Area 51 surrounds a test facility so secret the United States government won't even admit it exists!

It is here where highly classified national-security projects have been developed for several decades. And it is here where eyewitnesses on the fringe of Area 51 have seen and heard incredible flying objects zooming and darting in the sky.

Aviation experts believe the objects are super-secret spy planes undergoing flight tests. But some UFO researchers claim the objects are alien flying saucers captured by the military. At the very least, say these investigators, the objects are developed by the military from the technology learned from captured UFOs. And the investigators back their astounding claims with firsthand accounts—including a former government scientist who said he worked on one of the secret UFO projects.

Whatever they are, the bizarre craft have attracted curiosity-seekers and UFO believers to this desolate place, turning Area 51 into America's most popular secret spot. Night after night, people from all over the world come here, hoping to catch a glimpse of a spy plane, UFO, or human-piloted flying saucer.

Area 51 is actually a tract of land six miles wide by ten miles long (9.6 km by 16 km) connecting to the northeast corner of the military's Nevada Test Site about one hundred miles (160 km) north of Las Vegas. But people now refer to Area 51 as a much larger sector, including the military's entire restricted zone.

Ordinary citizens once were able to take a peek at the center of Area 51 from a vantage point known as Freedom Ridge, twelve miles (19 km) away. That was as close as civilians were allowed to go. But in April 1995, the government expanded its off-limits borders. Now the closest spot is about twenty-five miles (40 km) away on Tikaboo Peak, which requires an extremely challenging hike.

Before Freedom Ridge was restricted, viewers with telescopes could see the secret base nestled between steep mountains by the usually dry Groom Lake. The base features hundreds of small buildings, dozens of airplane hangars, satellite dishes, control towers, and two extremely long runways.

Area 51 is so secret that it doesn't appear on any Federal Aviation Administration or United States Geological Survey map. In fact, it doesn't even have an official name. In addition to Area 51 and Groom Lake, the base has several less formal nicknames, such as Dreamland (for the strange aircraft developed there), the Ranch, the Box, and Watertown Strip, to name just a few.

"It is perhaps the most secret military installation in American history," Donovan Webster wrote in the *New York Times Magazine*.

The base is protected by ground-motion detectors, heat sensors, high-powered infrared telescopes, digital-system radio frequencies, guard stations, and dome-shaped antennas that can detect a vehicle moving twenty-five miles (40 km) away. Lurking in the distance are what veteran viewers call "Cammo Dudes"—roving security agents wearing camouflage outfits and driving around in Jeep Cherokees.

In the desert surrounding Area 51 is a line of orange posts, some topped with stainless-steel globes the size of basketballs. Several closed-circuit TV cameras have been positioned as sentries. At those places and at other key locations around the desert are large signs that warn "Restricted Area." Go farther and you will see signs that also advise "Use of deadly force authorized."

Because air force and Pentagon officials continue to flatly deny the existence of the base, facts are hard to come by. However, the Pentagon admits that in 1954 the military secretly began developing new spy planes in the area. The first was the U-2, a high-altitude craft used to spy on Communist countries.

In later years, according to the *New York Times,* the base served as a laboratory for such top-secret aircraft as the SR-71 Blackbird spy plane, the B-2 Stealth bomber, and the F-117A Stealth fighter. The base also housed the "Red Hat Squadron," a stable of aircraft purchased from pilots who defected from, or left, the Soviet Union.

"Another rumor widely circulated is that the base has recently been home to an entirely new breed of supersonic spy plane called the Aurora," said the *Times.* "It is a triangular-shaped black aircraft that can fly up to eight times the speed of sound." People have heard a strange sonic boom that may have tripped a trail of earthquake sensors beneath its flight path over the Mojave Desert in June 1991. Other witnesses have described seeing a unique-looking contrail (the white trail of water vapor in a plane's wake) that resembles doughnuts on a rope.

Aurora—if it exists—is shrouded in deep secrecy. Although few people claim to have seen this plane, many say they have sensed its presence. Aurora is supposed to have an unusual sound: a very loud, deep, throbbing roar unlike any other aircraft.

During the base's first thirty-five years, local cowboys and miners would gather at the mailbox of rancher Steve Medlin, whose land touches Area 51. They would watch the blinding, fluttering lights of what they assumed were the test flights of secret spy planes. Other nights they stood and listened as sonic booms thundered and cracked from every angle in the sky and echoed through the canyons. But then there were times when they saw flying objects that left them in complete awe—like a silent whirling dome that appeared above the mountains and hovered in one place before hopscotching around the sky.

In recent years many observers have reported seeing strange flying objects over Area 51 performing in ways that no known aircraft possibly could. They fly at great speeds, stopping abruptly and hovering for periods of time. The early sightings were almost always at night. In a few cases witnesses saw the objects reflected in the moonlight and were able to determine that the craft resembled huge triangles.

In 1990, *Aviation Week & Space Technology* editor John D. Morrocco wrote that a "quantum leap in aviation" apparently had taken place under great secrecy.

Certain groups now believe that the technology that created the remarkable new aircraft came from aliens from another planet. According to this theory, the breakthrough emerged from studies of crashed extraterrestrial spacecraft that had been stored at the Area 51 base.

According to aviation writer James C. Goodall, who has investigated Area 51, "Rumor has it that some of these [power] systems involve force-field technology, gravity-drive systems, and 'flying saucer' designs. Rumor further has it that these designs are not necessarily of Earth origin."

Other writers and researchers have interviewed people who told of secret projects based on extraterrestrial technology. But none of these informants has offered proof.

The person attracting the most attention is Robert Scott Lazar, who in November 1989 appeared on a Las Vegas television news show. He said that he worked briefly for a secret government project analyzing the power source (also known as propulsion system) of alien flying saucers. On TV he showed government pay documents to prove that he worked at the secret base during the time that he claimed he did.

Lazar said that when he was hired, he didn't know what he would be working on, only that he would be doing something with "advanced propulsion systems." When he reported for work in Las Vegas, he was taken by plane and bus to a highly secure facility known as S-4, a few miles south of Groom Lake in Area 51. There he learned the true nature of his work—to "reverse-engineer" alien craft. In other words, he was to study the propulsion system of the alien craft to see how it worked, so the U.S. military could reproduce it for its new generation of planes.

Lazar claimed he saw nine flying saucers stored in camouflaged hangars near a spot in Area 51 known as Papoose Lake. The alien craft had either been captured or had crashed, but Lazar knew of no live aliens. He said he saw one of the captured UFOs fly briefly, piloted by air force personnel. He also said he examined one saucer in detail, studied military briefing documents on alien technology, and read government accounts of humans making contact with aliens.

Lazar claimed that while working in Area 51, he became aware that the alien craft's power source involved "a nearly unimaginable technology," involving an "antigravity reactor."

Lazar didn't last long on this secret project, in part because he couldn't resist talking to his friends about it. In fact, he even brought them to the edge of Area 51 so they could view the test flight of a saucer (piloted by a human). Within a few months of beginning work at the "secret saucer base," as he called it, Lazar was fired.

According to Lazar, no one in Congress knew anything about the project. He said he broke the secrecy because it was unlikely the government would ever announce the truth about the alien craft to the American people.

"There have long been rumors of alien craft at the Nevada Test Site and adjoining Nellis Range," said Glenn Campbell, who heads the Area 51 Research Center, a private organization seeking the truth behind the bizarre sightings in the Nevada desert. "But Lazar was the first to make specific firsthand public claims. His story has been impossible to confirm but also curiously difficult to [dispute].

"According to Lazar's claims, these saucers may be of alien origin, but they are currently housed and operated by humans. The alleged location was a good one—an off-limits area near Papoose Dry Lake—and no government agency seems willing to directly deny his claims. Even people who believe Lazar find it hard to make sense of it all. Where did the saucers come from? Why hasn't the public been told about them?

"Whatever you think about Lazar and his truthfulness, his story is consistent and disciplined enough for investigators to draw logical conclusions about how to proceed. If the government did have alien hardware in its possession, Area 51 or nearby areas in the Nellis Air Force Range or Nevada Test Site would be the logical place to keep them. Secrecy and security are impressive here, and no one who knows what is really going on is talking."

After Lazar's astounding television interview, UFO believers and researchers began arriving at the borders of Area 51, hoping to catch a glimpse of human-piloted alien craft. Then, when the Russians released a Soviet satellite photo of the Groom Lake base, news reporters showed up. All the attention turned the nearby hamlet of Rachel, Nevada—where about thirty families live in mobile homes—into a unique tourist destination. A roadhouse was remodeled into a restaurant-motel called the Little A'Le'Inn (little alien, get it?). In addition to the inn, the town has a gas station, convenience store, two RV parks, a Laundromat, and a headquarters for UFO believers and Area 51 investigators.

Most weekdays Rachel is bombarded by loud aircraft noise and many earth-shaking sonic booms, which sometimes knock pictures off the wall and send fragile family heirlooms flying off shelves. Rachel residents take it all in stride and hardly seem to notice the explosions and rumbles that send visitors running for cover.

During the last few years, so-called UFO experts have been leading tour groups to the area. Some claimed to have experienced bizarre encounters, like the one reported by Richard Boylan in the August 1992 issue of *Mufon UFO Journal*, a publication geared toward UFO believers.

Boylan, a clinical psychologist who conducted an expedition to Area 51, said that one night he saw an intensely burning gold light rise above the Groom Lake range. It hovered and glided slowly sideways. Whenever it moved, it glowed brighter. After four minutes, it slipped below the ridge line.

About a half hour later, another super-intense white light with bluish tones rose about 1,500 feet (457 m), hovered, and drifted to the left and then to the right. The craft began blinking and did a series of maneuvers that seemed to defy the laws of physics. Wrote Boylan:

"It jumped from one position to another, changing positions almost simultaneously over a distance of about 500 feet [152 m] in two-thirds of a second, in a crazy-quilt pattern of sideways, crisscrosses, and ups and downs, in a random tic-tac-toe kind of sequencing. The craft kept up these split-second gyrations for several minutes."

According to UFO researcher Sean Morton, who has visited the borders of Area 51 many times and conducted tours of the site:

"Probably the most amazing thing about Area 51 is the fact that this is literally the only place in the world where you can go out and actually see flying saucers on a timetable basis. You can literally go out there on a Wednesday night between about seven P.M. and one A.M., and you'll see these things flying up and down the valley. It's absolutely amazing. Even on a bad night, you'll have ten, eleven, twelve sightings. On a good night . . . the sky will just rip open with these things. You'll see anywhere between twenty to forty objects in a night testing over the base for anywhere from fifteen and forty minutes at a time."

Aviation experts, however, believe virtually all the sightings can be explained as satellites, shooting stars, and secret aircraft such as the Aurora.

NBC *Nightly News* aired a brief report on Area 51 on April 20, 1992. It included footage of a bright light that hovered over the mountains.

Reporter Fred Francis told the TV audience, "This is exclusive NBC news night-vision video of one of those secret flying machines. Not Aurora, but something that seems to defy the law of physics. Hundreds of witnesses have seen the bright light hovering motionless over mountains, then move quickly across the night sky at high speeds—like a flying saucer."

People continue to drive out to the edges of Area 51 along State Road 375, often known as "The Alien Highway" because of all the UFO sightings reported along this lonely stretch of pavement.

Glenn Campbell hopes that one day soon we'll learn the truth about Area 51. In the meantime he continues to write about eyewitness accounts in a newsletter called "Desert Rat"—which even the military reads!

Air Force Colonel Douglas Kennett told the *New York Times:* "We read his publication, and we know what Mr. Campbell is doing near a base that may—or may not—exist. While Mr. Campbell says the base is there, and while the Soviets appear to have photographed a base there, the Air Force is also aware of those times when Mr. Campbell or Russian spy satellites might be looking us over—and we can adjust our activities for that. That is, if any activities are going on at a base that may—or may not—exist."

Although the government does not officially acknowledge the base, because it's such a large facility and has one of the longest runways in the world, something secret must be undergoing tests there, said Campbell.

"If they [the air force] are trying to keep something out of the public eye, then it follows that you will have difficulty seeing it," said Campbell. "On the other hand, if they are testing a secret craft, then they have to fly it."

He added that a flying saucer like the kind Lazar

described, if there is one, would be an object that could change direction abruptly, travel up as easily as straight across, stop on a dime, take off again at high speed, and vanish from view in midair. The most common report from witnesses near Area 51 is of a bright object that appears to jump from one point to another in the sky in an instant.

"My own experiences neither prove nor disprove other people's sightings or the stories told by Lazar and other former workers about alien craft at or near Area 51," said Campbell. "These stories remain intriguing to me, and I see the mystery as far from solved.

"If you understand how the Groom Lake base can continue to 'not exist' in spite of all the obvious evidence to the contrary and how thousands of workers can be kept from talking about it, then you will see that almost anything could be kept secret here, even craft from other worlds."

THE MYRTLES PLANTATION

St. Francisville, Louisiana

No bed and breakfast inn in America seems more haunted than Louisiana's Myrtles Plantation.

Over the past two centuries the sprawling mansion has been the scene of at least ten violent deaths—many of them murders.

Apparently, the dear departed refuse to depart. Their spirits have made their presence felt long after their earthly remains were buried.

Among the phantoms startled witnesses have seen are two ghostly children who were poisoned, a Confederate soldier who was slain, and a barefoot slave girl who was hanged for murder.

Ghosts have even been photographed—and one picture taken of a wall shows an outstretched hand with no body.

Guests have heard ghostly music, children crying, and strange footsteps. They have smelled the unexplained scents of perfume, flowers, or pipe smoke in the rooms. Most chilling of all are the creepy touches from phantom hands that guests have felt while sitting on the veranda. Also unnerving are the times when guests awake to see their covers being pulled up over their shoulders by an invisible force.

A crystal chandelier will sometimes swing wildly for no apparent reason. A room will suddenly turn icy cold. A piece of furniture will move as though it had a mind of its own.

Owners of the bed and breakfast inn—located near St.

Francisville, Louisiana, forty miles (64 km) north of Baton Rouge—have re-created a house with all the richness and atmosphere of the Old South. Apparently, they succeeded in making The Myrtles so authentic that the ghosts of those who resided there in ages past feel both welcome and at home.

"I've personally experienced strange occurrences at the plantation," St. Francisville Police Captain Larry Peters told reporters. "The ghosts are doing them—there's no other explanation. It's definitely a haunted house."

And it's been that way for much of its history. The original owner may be to blame.

In 1796 David Bradford, who had been one of George Washington's generals during the Revolutionary War, left the army and moved to Louisiana. There he found a spot where he wanted to build his mansion. Unfortunately, it was the site of a sacred ancient Native American burial ground. But he cleared the land anyway and built his magnificent home, which was named after the many crape myrtle trees in the area.

Some people believe that when General Bradford violated the sacredness of the burial grounds, The Myrtles became cursed. But he lived out his life at the mansion without encountering any ghosts or experiencing any tragedy.

Others weren't so lucky.

When General Bradford died in 1818, he left the plantation to his daughter Sarah Mathilde and her husband, Judge Clarke Woodruffe. A few years later, after the birth of their three children, the most horrifying event in the history of the house unfolded.

One of the five hundred slaves who worked on the plantation was a curious teenage girl named Chloe. She liked to eavesdrop on the family's conversations. One day, Chloe was caught listening to a private conversation between the judge and his wife. The angered judge was determined to teach the slave a cruel lesson she would never forget. As her punishment, part of Chloe's ear was cut off. To cover her missing ear, she wore a green scarf pulled down low.

Chloe waited for the right moment to seek her revenge. Her chance came a few months later when she was ordered to bake a birthday cake for the Woodruffes' eldest daughter. Chloe made a beautifully decorated cake. But it contained a secret ingredient—deadly poison from the juice of boiled oleander leaves.

Tragically, Mrs. Woodruffe and two of her daughters died from eating the cake. When the other slaves learned that Chloe had committed the murders, they were outraged. They dragged Chloe off and hanged her from a huge oak tree at the corner of the house.

Ever since the deaths, it is said that the ghosts of Chloe and her victims have roamed the halls and grounds of The Myrtles.

"The slave girl and the two daughters are very strong ghosts here," said Frances Kermeen, who owned the bed and breakfast inn during the 1980s. "The daughters have been seen playing all around the house. And the girl in the green scarf can be found wandering about the house adjusting the mosquito nets and bed linens."

Sam Moore, a cameraman for WAFB-TV in nearby Baton Rouge, saw the girls' ghosts during a party at the plantation.

"I was in the parlor, and I just happened to glance out the window and saw two little girls," he recalled. "They were looking in, dressed in nightclothes, like they should have been in bed but had sneaked down to watch the party. I went outside and checked around, but they were gone."

Moore said the girls hadn't had time to run away when he got outside. "I'm absolutely convinced they were ghosts."

Kermeen had further proof that the girls' spirits exist. "The little girls have turned up in photographs taken by our guests on the plantation—even though the guests didn't see the girls at the time they were taking the pictures," she said.

Kermeen owns a mysterious photograph in which the faint faces and bodies of the two children can be seen. The picture was taken in the carriage room during a party while guests were singing by the piano. In the picture, the two ghostly girls are standing next to the piano.

In 1992 John and Teeta Moss bought The Myrtles. "When I first heard about the ghosts, I thought they were the greatest marketing ploy ever," said Teeta. "I wasn't a believer then." She is now.

The Mosses have shown guests several photos of The Myrtles' back porch, each shot from a different angle—and each showing the shadowy figure of a woman who some believe is Sarah Mathilde's ghost.

Several years after the triple murders, The Myrtles was sold, only to become the scene of more sorrow and death.

"During the Civil War," said Kermeen, "people at the plantation housed a deserter, a wounded Confederate soldier. But he was later killed after he was discovered at the plantation. Now, some people who spend the night in the room where the soldier stayed have vivid dreams about the Civil War. Some wake up to find a ghost servant bandaging their foot."

Another Confederate soldier died in one of the bedrooms. Ever since The Myrtles was turned into an inn, guests who stay in that room often report the smell of pipe smoke, even though no one in the house has a pipe. Guests also have seen the faint shadow of a tall bearded man in a Confederate uniform looking in from the outside through one of the room's windows.

The ghosts of three Union soldiers have also been spotted at the mansion. Accounts from the area reveal that these soldiers were slain on the grounds of The Myrtles during the Civil War.

After the war the mansion was sold to attorney William Winter and his wife, Sarah Matilda (whose name, eerily, was identical—except for the spelling—to that of Judge Woodruffe's poisoned wife). Murder and mystery continued to plague the glorious home.

One night, while Winter was in the parlor, he was called out onto the front porch by an unknown horseman. Seconds after Winter walked outside, shots were fired. Winter staggered back inside and, covered with blood, struggled up the main stairs of the house. He made it to the seventeenth step, where he died in his wife's arms.

Many nights since the unsolved murder, between eight and nine P.M., people in the house have heard footsteps climbing the staircase when no one is on the stairs. The sounds of the ghostly footsteps always stop at the seventeenth step, said Kermeen.

Over recent years, guests have reported seeing lighted candles in a holder floating up the stairway. Others have seen the wispy figure of a woman carrying the candle holder up the stairs. Some believe she is the ghost of Sarah Matilda Winter heading for the spot where her husband gasped his final breath.

The ghosts of two other murder victims reportedly show up at The Myrtles as well. One is that of a young man who was stabbed over a gambling debt. The other spirit belongs to a former overseer of the plantation. He was stabbed in a robbery attempt in 1927. "People see him dressed in work clothes," said Kermeen. "He's actually told tourists to go away."

Kermeen said she didn't know The Myrtles was haunted until after she had decided to buy it in 1980. The first night Kermeen spent in her "new" house, she thought she was alone. She was wrong. Kermeen awoke several times during the night to find that someone kept turning on the light in her room. She soon saw the ghost of an African-American girl in a green scarf—and later learned it was Chloe's wandering spirit.

Kermeen figured that if she was going to live in the house, she had to learn to accept the ghosts. It wasn't as bad as she thought it would be. The ghosts never threatened her. Quite the contrary. The Myrtles' ghosts have been rather friendly, even calling employees at the inn by their first names. Except for the few instances when the spirits have rearranged the furniture, they do very little to annoy people, Kermeen said.

Still, the ghosts like to make their presence known.

Guest Mike Cavanaugh told a reporter in 1994, "Last night on the veranda, I thought someone was tapping me on my shoulder, but no one was there. Then this morning when we got up, there was a strong scent of roses in the room. But there were no roses around. I asked my wife if she had perfume on, but she didn't. We both smelled them, though, real strong."

Another guest reported in a local magazine that during a night at the inn, her husband felt his ring get so hot that it burned his finger. Meanwhile, she dreamed of a little red-headed girl who wanted to get into their high four-poster bed. "She begged me to tell the owners [of the inn] to put children's furniture back in the house, because there was no place comfortable for her to sit or sleep," said the guest.

Visitors have seen a Native American ghost at the pond behind the house. They've also spotted a big dog with blue eyes that disappears right in front of them when they come too close.

The ghost of a French woman wanders around the place as if she's looking for someone. Cries of an infant can be heard coming from the room where a child died long ago. Some believe the French woman is looking for the baby to comfort.

Guests also have reported seeing a phantom girl peering into one of the windows. She appears suddenly from nowhere, usually in the middle of a storm, and then vanishes.

The Myrtles' historian, Bill Pohlman, has reported that people at the inn have heard ghostly music such as a string quartet, violins, harpsichord, and piano. All the music appears to be coming from the piano. "Naturally, it's impossible for this instrument to produce those sounds other than piano," Pohlman said.

In another part of the house, a bizarre painting of an unknown man has caused people to faint from fright. They claim the man in the portrait can change his expression from a smile to an evil frown. It's so creepy that when a photograph was taken of the painting, a faint, bloody, grasping hand mysteriously appeared in the photo.

Police Captain Larry Peters said that in 1987 several people reported seeing a woman in a long white dress walk across the front yard of the mansion before vanishing a split second later.

He claimed he personally has seen two weird sights at The Myrtles.

"One night I went out to the plantation, and a lady's car was going crazy—the locks were going up and down, the trunk would open and shut, and the lights were going on and off," he said.

"On Halloween night in 1986, I went into a room there, and when I started back out, the doorknob had disappeared. Then it was later found in a drawer in another room."

In 1983 a group of five psychics from the Baton Rouge area spent the night at The Myrtles to investigate the strange happenings there.

From the moment the psychics walked in the front door, they began having close encounters with "layer upon layer of spirits," according to an account of the evening.

"I just heard a series of thumps coming from the staircase, and then suddenly they stopped," one of the psychics told the group.

Another psychic started walking up the staircase, pointed to one of the steps, and exclaimed, "Something terrible happened here!" She was pointing to the seventeenth step where William Winter had died after being shot.

Other members of the group began to sense the energy fields of the spirits. "They keep scooting off," said a psychic. "I guess they're timid or a bit annoyed that we are crowding their territory."

"Here's one that isn't," said a fellow psychic, stretching his hands toward a spot at the foot of the stairway, directly in front of the entranceway. "He's big and strong—perhaps six feet six [2 m]. I suspect he was a servant who was assigned during his lifetime to remain at this station. Come feel here— he has a particularly strong vibration."

Joanie Fitzgerald, who was escorting the group on a tour of the home, stepped forward. To her surprise, she felt a tingling sensation in her fingers when she reached for the spot where the spirit stood.

Marcia Westerfield-Willis, editor of the local publication *Feliciana Journal,* who didn't believe in ghosts, had come to report on the psychics' visit. She thrust her hand out, but very quickly pulled it back. "Ouch!" she shouted. "I felt a shock like I get from my hair dryer."

The psychic team continued to inspect the rooms in the

house and noticed that the spirits were beginning to warm up to them. "They are now coming forward to investigate us intruders to see if we are friend or foe," said one of the psychics.

"Something just patted me on the head," a fellow psychic announced. A colleague then reported being touched on the upper arm by a cold, clammy, invisible hand.

Walking into one of the upstairs bedrooms, several in the group detected the spirit of a little girl jumping up and down on the bed. Joanie wasn't surprised. "This used to be the nursery where the children slept," she said.

The psychics decided to hold a group meditation session in the room. As they sat in a circle and began clearing their minds, one of them exclaimed, "That little girl is now sitting next to me fooling with my mustache."

Another said, "I'm getting a reading from a spirit that says, 'Forget about the little girl!' This new spirit says her name is Josepha, but that she prefers to be called Bethie. She says her father imprisoned her in this room."

The group members focused their energies upon Bethie to learn more about her troubles. Her father, they were told, wanted to keep her apart from the man she loved so that the father could force her to marry someone more to his liking. When her true love came to her rescue, he was captured by servants and severely beaten.

Bethie became particularly attached to one of the members of the psychic group and refused to let go of him once she told her story. "I'm not spending the night in here," he said as he fled into the next room.

The psychics then crawled into their sleeping bags on the floor of another room, turned out the lights, and tried to go to sleep. "I can't shut this door," complained one of the psychics. "Something is keeping it from closing."

"The chair in the corner just moved," said another.

"What's that smell?" asked a third psychic.

"It's the gardenia-scented perfume Bethie wears," one of them replied. "She has come looking for us."

Despite the ghostly encounters, the psychics finally fell asleep. But they were awakened at one-forty A.M. by a thunderous crash. An ice chest had been lifted several feet off the floor and then dropped. "I guess the spirits don't want us to go to sleep yet," said a psychic. "There must be more thrills in store for us."

Indeed there were. Not long after that, the group watched in amazement as glowing wisps of colorful lights danced around the room for several minutes. The psychics assumed the lights were energy radiating from the spirits.

The group came away believing that the unfortunate spirits who met their untimely deaths at the plantation will remain there, destined to roam The Myrtles forever.

AMERICA'S STONEHENGE
North Salem, New Hampshire

England has its Stonehenge . . . and so does the United States.

America's Stonehenge doesn't look much like England's famous ring of towering ancient stones, which stand on an open plain visible for miles around. The American ruins are much smaller and more crude in construction and are hidden among the woods.

However, America's Stonehenge has its own strange flair. The astonishing complex of stone structures and walls was built by human hands thousands of years ago for some unexplained purpose. No one knows who these ancient builders were or why they built it.

Located on a high wooded area known as Mystery Hill near North Salem, New Hampshire, forty miles (64 km) north of Boston, the complex is one of the largest and possibly the oldest of the stone-built sites in North America. Since its discovery, it has puzzled archaeologists, astronomers, and historians as well as tourists of all ages.

America's Stonehenge consists of dark little stone-walled caverns, mysterious cellar holes, and great slabs of stone scarred with shallow V-shaped marks. Entrances lead into eerie chambers and curious little niches and cubbyholes.

All twenty-two structures are made of bare granite stone, tightly fitted, many with large boulders as roofs. Some of the stones are huge, especially the roof slabs, which weigh up to eleven tons. It would take about one hundred strong people to lift these rocks so neatly into place.

Researchers have discovered that these stones were used to make shrines, cupboards, tombs, chambers, wells, storerooms, guardhouses, and a remarkable system of stone-lined underground drains. Everything was built on a scale for people much shorter and smaller than modern-day Americans.

The single most bizarre structure is the "sacrificial table." This large, bell-shaped, five-ton slab of stone rests on four stone legs and looks like a giant butcher's cutting board. It even has a shallow groove that runs inside all four edges and connects to a gutter. The table is slightly angled so that any liquid collected in the groove will drain off through the gutter into a hollowed-out area of bedrock.

What kind of liquid dripped from the stone? Experts think blood from the sacrifice of an animal—or possibly even a human. Animal sacrifices certainly seem to be a possibility, because a small stone pen big enough to hold a couple of goats, lambs, or pigs is close to the table.

A ramp slopes up to a retaining wall directly in front of the sacrificial table. Facing toward the rising sun, the ramp is large enough to hold spectators, possibly worshippers.

Another weird feature is the "speaking tube," a small pipelike tunnel under the table leading back through eight feet (2.4 m) of rock into a large chamber directly behind the table. The underground chamber, twenty-two feet (6.7 m) long and six and a half feet (2 m) high, holds a stone seat and has a secret narrow passageway that experts think was used by an ancient mystic or seer.

Hidden inside the chamber, the seer would speak into the tube and project his voice to the outside. To those people sitting on the ramp in front of the sacrificial table, it would sound like an eerie voice coming from deep underground. Since they couldn't see the opening of the tube directly under the table, they likely believed that the voice came from a god—possibly the one to whom a sacrifice had been made on that very table.

Nearby is another crudely built chamber less than three feet (1 m) high. It is reached by a passage covered with heavy slabs of stone, which also leads to several other low chambers. Strangely, according to some experts, simple carvings on these stones seem to show a bull and a horned gazelle—animals unknown in North America at the time the carvings were made.

Like Stonehenge in England, this stone complex was built by ancient people who knew astronomy and stone construction. Scientists who have studied the site believe it is a very large and accurate astronomical calendar. It can determine specific events of the moon and the sun during the year.

Researchers discovered that when they looked from behind the sacrificial table, the walls and certain large slabs of stone marked out the true points of the compass. At certain times of the year, these stones also marked the solstices (when the sun reaches the points farthest north and south) and equinoxes (when the sun reaches the equator, making night and day of equal length).

Writer Arthur Goldsmith described the awesome feeling of experiencing America's Stonehenge on the winter solstice: "Sitting alone on that New Hampshire hilltop, I watched the sun setting behind the trees. Directly ahead of me, down an alley where the trees have been cleared away, was the Winter Solstice Monolith [a large stone], like a black shark's tooth against the afternoon sky. A single fat stone located in one of the surrounding stone walls, it is placed so that the sun, when viewed from the center of the main complex, sets directly behind it during the shortest day of the year. A few hundred feet north is a marker for the summer solstice. Other shrines and markers . . . are stone dials that clock the equinox, the rising sun on midsummer's day, and other astronomical events. All around me lay the silent evidence of something extraordinary."

Who built the many chambers and structures with huge stones atop Mystery Hill? Who went to such painstaking care to shape each standing stone and place it in its exact location to mark an important event of the sky? And why did they carry out all this back-breaking work?

Researchers are sure of one thing: America's Stonehenge was built by people who were here long before Christopher Columbus arrived in the New World in 1492.

Archaeologists digging at the site have uncovered prehistoric artifacts, stone tools, and pottery that are four thousand years old! The mysterious structures may be far older than those in ancient Rome or Greece.

Scientists have unearthed several thousand man-made objects dating back to many periods and cultures. The carvings in different languages could mean that America's Stonehenge was known as an astronomical observatory and ceremonial center and used by travelers from various cultures at different times over the centuries.

The site is likely "to drive an archaeologist frantic with frustration," said scientist Andrew Rothovius. Scholars say there are similarities between these ruins and those in western Europe dating back to 1500 B.C. Speaking tubes like the one hidden under the sacrificial table have been found in ancient sites throughout Europe.

Despite half a century of investigation, no one has yet determined for sure who created America's Stonehenge.

Some experts believe the stones are the remains of a Viking settlement. Others say it was a tenth-century monastery built by Irish monks who sailed to North America to escape Viking raids on their homeland. Still others think it was an ancient temple created by visiting Europeans between 800 B.C. and A.D. 300.

In 1975 Harvard professor Dr. Barry Fell, an expert on ancient languages, examined carvings that had been chiselled into the stones on Mystery Hill. Some were in an ancient language used long ago by the Celtic people, whose territories stretched from the Scottish Highlands in the north to as far south as Spain.

Author Andre Norton suggested that the site may have been a settlement of ancient people who lived on the other side of the Atlantic Ocean in a Mediterranean region known as Phoenicia. In 335 B.C., Greek philosopher Aristotle made a list of 178 marvels. According to Norton, Aristotle named as item eighty-four a mysterious overseas land the Phoenicians kept a strict secret because of trade. "His description," said Norton, "might well be that of [America's Stonehenge on] Mystery Hill."

But why would these travelers march inland for twenty-five miles (40 km) to construct such a site? No one knows. The local woodland Native Americans probably would not have allowed foreigners to settle among them. Yet scientists say it's unlikely that the Native Americans built America's Stonehenge, because tribes back then didn't build with stone.

Researcher Virgil Anderson offered a far-out theory scoffed at by most scientists. He believed the massive stone structures were built as "a landing beacon or giant map for visiting extraterrestrials."

Said Anderson, "Mysterious hieroglyphics on some of the stones suggest visitations by beings far different from the

Native Americans who inhabited that portion of the country. But apparently the site was abandoned long before the arrival of white settlers.

"It's impossible to confirm this absolutely, of course. But if it's true, [the complex at] Mystery Hill is one of the most astounding examples of UFO visitation in the world. And maybe, just maybe, the aliens who built it will come back."

It's doubtful scientists will ever learn the truth, because much of the original site was destroyed by colonists and farmers over the last three hundred years. The main complex of structures was a jumble of gray stones and boulders. Much of the damage to the site was done during the 1800s when the land was owned by farmer Jonathan Pattee. In 1823 he built a frame house over a section of ancient stonework, which he used as a foundation. He sold off many rock slabs to builders in the nearby town of Lawrence, Massachusetts.

The first printed record of the site was penned in 1907 by Edgar Gilbert in his book *History of Salem*. He described America's Stonehenge as "a wild and beautiful spot among rough boulders and soft pines, about which the most weird and fantastic tales might be woven."

That still holds true today.

GENERAL WAYNE INN
Merion, Pennsylvania

The General Wayne Inn—the oldest continuously operated restaurant in the United States—is haunted by at least fifteen ghosts, including many who love to pull pranks.

"They're a lot of fun," said Bart Johnson, who owned the restaurant from 1970 to 1995. "They're always doing something. It's almost a nightly occurrence."

Johnson said the fun-loving ghosts have done everything from blow in customers' ears to fill the cash register with water. Chandeliers swing for no reason, glasses shake on the shelves, and electric lights dim, then go bright. Napkins, silverware, and glasses on the tables mysteriously get rearranged.

According to investigators with the Ghost Research Society and local psychics, the ghosts include several Revolutionary War soldiers, barmaids and customers from the 1800s, a young girl, and a sea captain.

The General Wayne Inn has been an outstanding landmark in the Philadelphia suburb of Merion, Pennsylvania, ever since it was built in 1704. After operating under several different names, it got its present name after a visit in 1795 by war hero Major General Anthony Wayne.

Among other important visitors who reportedly stayed there when it was an overnight inn were Benjamin Franklin and George Washington. Author Edgar Allan Poe visited the place in 1839 and 1843. It was here that he wrote and edited several stanzas of his most famous poem, "The Raven."

Over the years the building has been a post office, a coach stop, a barracks for soldiers in both the Revolutionary War and the Civil War, a central meeting place, and now a well-known restaurant—one filled with ghosts.

One of the spirits enjoys having a little fun with women customers. "He likes to go from one woman to another and blow in their ears," said Johnson. "Naturally, the ladies are startled and will blame innocent patrons.

"Many times, in a whole row of customers, each woman will turn to the man next to her and ask, 'Why did you blow in my ear?'"

According to investigators, the ghost was a soldier for hire during the Revolutionary War. He had annoyed so many women guests at the inn that he triggered a fight with several men and was killed.

Although Johnson said he's never actually seen a ghost, he has felt their presence "hundreds of times." And he and his family have often been the target of the ghosts' practical jokes.

"Once, I was relaxing on a stool after a busy evening," he recalled. "It was late, and everyone had left except for two elderly women friends. We were having coffee and talking when all of a sudden, a cannonball about the size of a tennis ball dropped from the ceiling."

It landed with a heavy thud about fifteen feet (4.6 m) in front of the stunned trio and then rolled slowly across the room toward them. After recovering from his shock, Johnson got off his stool and reached for the ball. To his disbelief, the ball disappeared.

"We checked the ceiling and found no holes," he said. "We looked all around the dining room, but we couldn't find the ball. Where the ball came from or why it happened, I don't know. There is no rhyme or reason for what the ghosts do.

"For example, one morning I entered the bar area and found the drawer to the cash register was full of water. So were many glasses and carafes [glass bottles for holding water or wine]. Who knows why?"

Several years ago, all twelve hundred glasses in the racks over the bar unexplainably began to shake, touching and clinking against each other without breaking. The bizarre shaking stopped after about five minutes. It happened again almost daily for a few months before stopping. "We looked for a cause, but never found one," said Johnson.

One evening, after all the visitors had left, the staff set the tables for the next day. The napkins, silverware, and glasses were all in their proper places. "The next morning, I walked in and every single napkin had been unfolded and tossed on the floor," Johnson recalled.

On another night, a customer drove up to the inn in a luxury car but refused to leave it with the valet, choosing to park the car himself and keep the keys with him. Partway through dinner, the valet ran into the inn and asked the owner of the car to come outside. To everyone's astonishment, the engine was running, the car lights and windshield wipers were on, and the stereo and horn were blaring.

The ghosts have also had fun at the expense of Johnson's wife, Dottie. In 1984 she went to the third-floor office of the inn to help out with the bookkeeping. As she totalled up the receipts using an old adding machine, she became bewildered because the machine kept coming up with wrong answers. Every time she totalled the same receipts, the adding machine gave a different answer. But every time she added the numbers by hand, she arrived at the same total.

"I tried the old machine and it was way off," Johnson recalled. "So I went out and bought her a calculator. And that one wouldn't work right either. It kept giving us the wrong answers. We knew that both devices couldn't be wrong. That was too much of a coincidence.

"Dottie wondered if ghosts were playing with her. After all, the place is haunted. So she got up from her desk, opened the door, and moved to the side. She faced the room and said in a stern voice, 'Look, fellahs, you all have to leave! I have work to do. Now, go on, get out of here.'"

Then Dottie closed the door and returned to her desk. She added the receipts again with the help of the calculator. This time, it gave the right answer. She did it again and found the calculator gave the same correct total. Then she tried the old adding machine. It worked accurately, too.

Not all the ghosts are pranksters. Several are the lost spirits of Hessians from the Revolutionary War, according to psychics, who have visited the General Wayne Inn.

During the war, the Hessians from Germany were hired by the British and brought to America to fight the colonists. Ghosts of Hessians have been seen for years throughout the restaurant.

One Sunday morning at the inn, Johnson noticed that the cleaning man had not finished his job and was nowhere to be found. Part of the main room had been carefully swept. The trash had been brushed into piles halfway across the room. Chairs and tables on the clean side were all in their proper place ready for setting. But the rest of the room and the bar area were a mess.

Johnson then called the cleaning man's home and was surprised when the man answered the phone. Johnson asked him why he had left work and when he would return.

"I'm not coming back today," said the cleaning man. "No, sir, no way. When I was about half done in the dining room, a noise made me look up. There in the far corner was standing a big soldier in one of those old-fashioned uniforms. He was just looking at me. So I put down my broom, put on my coat, and walked out."

According to Elizabeth Hoffman, author of *In Search of Ghosts: Haunted Places in the Delaware Valley,* noted psychic Jean Quinn discovered the identity of the soldier.

Quinn visited the inn, where she felt the presence of many spirits. One night when the inn was closed, she held a seance in a second-floor room. Moments after the group started, the two doors to the room unexplainably opened on their own.

Quinn was convinced it was a ghost. "We welcome you," she said. "We're glad you're here. Tell us your name."

Through the psychic, the spirit replied, "Wilhelm." He then explained that he and his fellow soldiers had been stationed at the inn during the Revolutionary War. One night, even though it was late, he went for a walk. A short distance from the building, he was ambushed by colonists and killed.

The next day a search party found his body and brought it back to the inn, where they dug a grave nearby. But before Wilhelm's body was buried, his commanding officer noticed that the boots and uniform of the dead soldier were in good condition. Following the officer's orders, a fellow soldier removed Wilhelm's clothes and replaced them with his own worn clothes.

In the séance, Wilhelm told the psychic that he had remained all these years at the inn because he was still looking for his clothes.

In 1990 a business group held a Christmas party at the inn. Later, a man told Johnson how much he enjoyed the party—especially the unique touch.

When Johnson asked what he meant by that, the man replied, "Why, the Hessian soldier. He walked all around, smiled and mingled with groups, and then moved on. We all thought that was a clever touch in this old place."

But no one at the inn or with the group had hired anyone to act the role of the soldier. No one knew who he was. "It was probably another one of those Hessian ghosts," said Johnson.

The spirit of a Hessian who died at the inn is often heard coughing and moaning in the basement, especially in the winter and on windy nights.

"We hear a lot of strange things in the basement," said Johnson. "I think a lot of ghosts hang out there."

Employees believe the moaning is from the ghost of a Hessian soldier named Hans who died there from pneumonia during the bitter winter of 1777.

Shortly before his death, he and his comrades were marching into Merion when they saw the inn. Exhausted, tired, and hungry, they beat on the door. The innkeeper was a Tory—a colonist who supported the British—so he let the Hessians enter and gave them food and drink.

Because every room was taken for that night, the innkeeper led the soldiers to the cellar and provided them with warm blankets. This was the first real shelter they had found in days. Grateful, they fell into a deep sleep.

But Hans couldn't sleep. He was in pain and burning with fever from his deadly disease. The next morning, his fellow soldiers knew there was no way he could continue the journey. They left, promising Hans they would return.

The innkeeper intended to check on Hans and find a doctor. But as the day wore on, the innkeeper became so busy that he forgot about Hans. By nightfall, Hans had died. His ghost, apparently, continues to cough and groan.

A phantom British officer has made several appearances at the restaurant, as well. During the Revolutionary War, he was shot in a battle and was carried into the inn. Clutched in his hand was a locket containing a miniature picture of a young woman. The officer died and was buried in the

Strangers Yard of the Merion Meeting burial ground next to the inn.

The identity of the officer was never learned, and the locket couldn't be returned to his family. Over the years, a sad-faced ghost in a British officer's uniform has been spotted walking the halls asking for his locket.

For an unknown reason, at least one ghost from the inn haunted a man from another town more than one hundred miles (160 km) away.

According to Johnson, in 1978 businessman Mike Benio from a suburb of Scranton, Pennsylvania, claimed he was awakened for several nights in a row by the ghost of a Hessian soldier sitting on his bed. The spirit said that he was from the General Wayne Inn and that he needed help.

While he was stationed at the inn, the spirit told Benio, he was killed by colonists and buried inside one of the thick walls of the inn. The Hessian's ghost wanted a proper burial.

When Benio realized he would never get a full night's rest unless he helped the ghost, Benio traveled to Merion and told Johnson about the ghostly encounters with the Hessian spirit.

"His story was hard to believe," Johnson recalled. "But anything is possible. Mike asked me for permission to try to find the soldier's bones, so I agreed."

Workers began digging in a basement wall, hauling up dirt and debris in buckets. When the material was sifted through a screen, human bone fragments were found. "It's obvious that at least one person had been buried in the basement," said Johnson. "As far as I know, the Hessian ghost stopped visiting Mike."

Many spirits other than soldiers continue to haunt the General Wayne Inn.

"There are a couple of ghosts of barmaids from the 1800s," said Johnson. "Through a psychic they talked about a traveling rug salesman who had arrived at the inn by horse and wagon. He was supposed to meet a wealthy customer. When the customer failed to show up, the salesman left his expensive rugs behind and went looking for him. The salesman never returned, and the rugs eventually were stolen. The two women spirits told the psychic that they were blamed for taking the rugs even though they were innocent."

During the séance with psychic Jean Quinn, several spirits wanted to be heard. One spoke German (the language of the Hessians). Another became hysterical and then faded away. A third was a little boy searching for his mother. Two others spoke briefly but were unclear about their reasons for haunting the inn.

Dale Kaczmarek, who heads the Ghost Research Society, tried what he called spirit photography at the inn in 1990. "We used very sensitive film and an infrared camera to take pictures in the dining room, where most of the ghost activity seems to take place," he explained. "This kind of photography can often capture things you can't see with the naked eye.

"When the film was developed, we found strange light formations. It appears to be energy coming out from the tables toward the walls."

Kaczmarek said the film and camera were examined by experts. The film also underwent computer enhancement. "The light was not caused by a problem with the camera or the film," he declared.

Kaczmarek said he has seen these strange light formations in other photographs that he has taken in places that reportedly are haunted.

"The ghosts at the inn aren't out to scare anyone," said Johnson. "They like to hang out. I just wish I could understand why they do some of the things they do."

CHACO CANYON

New Mexico

I n the northwest corner of New Mexico lies Chaco
Canyon—breathtaking Native American ruins that many
visitors believe hold mystical powers.

People from all walks of life have reported having bizarre
experiences where objects appear to change color, time seems
to slow down, bodies feel like they're vibrating, and visions
of ancient life pop into their minds.

Many centuries ago Chaco Canyon was the capital for a
group of Native Americans called the Anasazi (ah-nah-SAH-
zee). We don't know what they called themselves, but the
name means "Ancient Ones" or "Ancestors of the Alien
People" in some Native American languages.

For more than two thousand years the Anasazi lived in the
Four Corners region of the desert southwest—the area where
the states of Colorado, New Mexico, Arizona, and Utah meet.
The Anasazi hunted antelope, deer, and bighorn sheep with
spears and darts. They collected nuts, cactus, fruit, and berries
by the basketful. By A.D. 500 they began making pottery and
planting crops.

Up to the tenth century, most of their settlements were
hamlets of fewer than a hundred people. But then a new way
of life began. Archaeologists call it the Chaco Phenomenon.
About 150 Anasazi villages joined together to share their
traditions and way of life in a culture that stretched 250 miles
(400 km) from north to south.

Chaco Canyon became a large ceremonial and agricultural center with the surrounding settlements connected by more than two hundred miles (320 km) of wide roads. Pilgrims and peddlers were greeted from far and wide. Many archaeologists believe Chaco was a peaceful civilization led by astronomers, priests, tradesmen, and governors whose people gathered and shared food according to who needed it.

The Anasazi at Chaco lived in structures five stories tall, some containing hundreds of rooms built around airy plazas. The Anasazi were superb builders. Every stone was placed with care, every doorway was straight and true. The buildings were designed to capture the sun's rays and keep their residents warm and comfortable throughout the cool nights of fall and winter. The structures were often built under overhanging cliffs to offer shade during the hot summer.

The Chaco Phenomenon created an amazing system of roads—the Anasazi's version of our modern freeways and interstates—that stretched at least two hundred miles (320 km). What made them so remarkable was that these roads, thirty feet (9 m) wide, went for miles in dead-straight lines regardless of the shape of the land. Even over steep areas, the roads remained straight, with ramps and stairs sometimes cut right into stone.

The roads—many of which are still visible today—pose a great puzzle: Why would people who had no vehicles, no beasts of burden such as horses or mules, need highways?

Some experts think the roads were used by laborers who carried tens of thousands of heavy roof beams of ponderosa pine. The trees, from as far as eighty miles (128 km) away, were felled and trimmed with stone axes to build great houses. Other scholars think the roads were routes that pilgrims would follow to Chaco for religious ceremonies.

Based on the ruins of towers and lookout posts that line the roadways, some authorities believe the roads were built to be used by armies from Chaco.

For all its power, the Chaco Phenomenon lasted less than three hundred years. Something happened in the thirteenth century that forced most of the Anasazi from mesa tops and valley bottoms into new villages and cliff dwellings in Arizona and Colorado. Most of the canyon was abandoned. Then, just as strangely, around A.D. 1400, the Anasazi suddenly deserted half their empire. Why Chaco fell remains a mystery. Scholars suspect that the Anasazi left because of drought, famine, disease, or possibly attacks from hostile tribes.

The creepiest thing about their leaving is that many of the Anasazi left their belongings as though they would be back later that day. But they never returned.

Because of the dry air and the way their houses protected their possessions, many of their baskets, clothing, and other items have survived over the centuries.

Today the impressive ruins of Chaco Canyon stand in quiet tribute to the mysterious Anasazi. The remains of Chaco's hub are called Pueblo Bonito. This site lies below a 150-foot (47-m) cliff. The builders created at least seven hundred rooms into a design shaped like a huge capital D when seen from the air. A spacious plaza is bordered by thirty-seven circular underground chambers called kivas, which were used for religious purposes. Built without the use of compasses, one of the largest kivas is perfectly aligned with north-south.

"Their architecture was both graceful and functional," said Natasha Peterson, author of *Sacred Sites*. "It is also undeniably futuristic. Looking at any painting of what Pueblo Bonito in Chaco probably was like in its heyday is like looking at a . . . twenty-second-century space station."

Chaco Canyon—officially known as Chaco Culture National Historical Park—is about 140 miles (224 km) northwest of Albuquerque, New Mexico. The site is so isolated that the nearest town is sixty miles (96 km) away. To get there requires driving twenty miles (32 km) up a steep grade on a dirt road. But Chaco Canyon is definitely worth the trip, say visitors.

"The ruins blend so completely with the land that you cannot make them out until you are quite close," said Peterson. "When they do appear, they are like an optical illusion that comes into focus."

Time has a way of becoming distorted for visitors, she said. "Timelessness is often a part of experiencing Chaco Canyon. . . . Here you are surrounded for miles by Anasaziland, stepping into their perfectly circular kivas, treading their pathways, walking through their doorways, seeing the sky, and breathing the air as they did. On the breeze at Chaco, you can soon hear bells and instruments, the cries of children, the grinding of corn, and the chatter of folk at work. With the sundown comes the low chant of the Anasazi at prayer as fires are lit in the kivas. Past and present merge. Their spirits still [remain in] Chaco Canyon."

Some visitors describe overwhelming feelings and sensations that defy understanding.

"Walking into one of the rooms, I felt an overpowering feeling," said a New York stockbroker. "It's like nothing I've ever experienced before—sort of like I was entering a dream that belonged to someone who had lived a thousand years ago."

Added a teenager from Florida, "I felt light-headed walking in Chaco. My whole body tingled. It was cool."

A regular visitor, who along with his wife has been to Chaco more than a dozen times, said, "This is our favorite place. Once you see it, if you have any curiosity at all, you've got to see more. We are fascinated by its mystery."

That's no surprise to Native American Jose Lucero. "People come from all over because of the way they feel here in the Four Corners region," he said. "It has always been a sacred place for the Hopi and Navajo.

"There are special things all around us, but sometimes we have to work hard to begin to see them."

People have seen weird flashing lights and heard strange popping and sizzling sounds. To some believers, this proves that it's a sacred site where visitors feed off the energy of the spirits of the Anasazi.

However, some scholars suspect that these visions are triggered by an energy force from Earth known as electro-magnetism.

Earth is a giant magnet that puts out shifting amounts of energy. This magnetic shield sets the compass and protects Earth from radiation from space. It also has a major effect on living things, said Dr. Robert Becker, author of *The Body Electric*. "In the past decade, we've just begun to understand that we're creatures of the Earth's magnetic field."

He told about the time some vacationers fled from a remote valley near Chaco Canyon when they thought they saw objects change color. For example, to them, dozens of cactus looked red instead of green. Of course, the cactus hadn't really changed color—except in their minds.

That's because disturbances in Earth's electromagnetic field sometimes occur in a particular area such as Chaco Canyon. These very sharp changes can affect a person's brain. "As a result," said Dr. Becker, "he experiences unpredictable psychological effects, like bizarre color perceptions—maybe even mystical visions."

During a camping trip in Anasaziland, a man named

Chuck told author Natasha Peterson: "I suddenly realized that I felt a little lighter, like the clouds over me had lifted a little. I walked up to a nearby Indian ruin, and the moonlight was very bright. The coyotes were singing everywhere. I sat near the ruin, and in a joking, sarcastic way, I said, 'Okay, show me the magic.'

"Immediately, instantly from the distance a loud, sharp, buzzing noise came right at me and flew past me. I broke out in goose bumps. I'd never felt or heard anything like it. I looked up and saw this image, I guess you could say ghost, but it was different. I saw this four-foot (1.2-m) tall medicine man doing this fast, outrageous dance. I picked up feelings immediately that he was frightened, but also angry at me. I felt that I was invading his world. I looked away and back, and he was still there. I closed my eyes, and when I opened them he was gone. I figured my imagination was in top form and returned to my tent."

· The next day Chuck went into town and bought a book about sacred places. That's when he realized that many people have strange experiences there.

"We're electrical beings living in a magnetic environment," scientist Louis Slesin told *Psychology Today* magazine. We're finely tuned to energy fields that we normally can't feel. But when this energy is especially strong, as it apparently is at Chaco Canyon, our bodies and minds can feel the change and react in unusual ways.

For example, here's one woman's description of her experience: "The sensation for me was vibration in the air like a light tapping or brushing against your skin. As we walked around, we began to feel a little dizzy. I can't explain it. The pull of gravity was less. . . . It was marvelous, though, and we felt great—almost walking without our feet touching the ground. And our bodies felt transparent. We could feel the

68

energy going through us, in and then out again, not just around us. It was a very strong force. Quite thrilling."

What the visitor brings to the sacred place is as important as what he gets from it, said Dr. James Swan, president of the Institute for the Study of Natural Systems. "The natural world really does talk back to us sometimes, but not in the Disney sense."

"Visitors to such sacred sites should become more aware of what they are feeling," said Jose Lucero.

"Our [Native American] ancestors, who not all that long ago beat drums, danced around the fire, and talked to animals, could describe certain feelings, like the ones that come from sacred places, better than we can. Some might think that sounds foolish, but the really foolish thing would be to abandon that ten thousand years of wisdom."

"Sacred sites such as Chaco Canyon have put young people in touch with their ancient ancestors," said Lucero. "When our young people say they've lost feeling for our traditions, we tell them, 'You've been lazy. Go get your drum—that's the heartbeat that regulates us.' When they listen to the elders drum and sing, it's like they hit 'recall'—the kids suddenly remember dances from a hundred years before they were born.

"For some things you can't just watch the video. You have to have the experience."

"Some people believe Chaco Canyon is a sacred site because they dreamed about it long before they ever visited it. In the same way we are attracted to different people, so too are we attracted to different places," said Peterson. "Certain places on Earth light up for us as surely as certain individuals do."

Past civilizations often built their temples and ceremonial centers in areas where highly sensitive priests and leaders felt the Earth's energy. That's why energy is so often felt at a site such as Chaco Canyon.

In fact, the Anasazi may have chosen that site because they were influenced by an even earlier civilization from that area. Based on stunning rock art in outlying cliff shelters, archaeologists believe that people once lived there as far back as four thousand years ago.

On many of the ancient rock paintings and carvings are painted handprints—a sign believed to mark the art as a sacred image or a spiritual bridge to the supernatural. The rock art features religious symbols found throughout the Anasazi world. Besides humans, the rock art shows animals, lizards, serpents, flute players, women giving birth, and strange creatures that experts still can't identify.

"Sacred sites . . . often display powerful evidence of the advanced and sometimes startling capabilities of ancient cultures," said Peterson. "These mysteries include lost civilizations, visits by spirit guides, and possibly extra-terrestrials. . . . Unfortunately, the bright lights of their wisdom still only glimmer for us as most of their messages have yet to be [solved]. Nevertheless, even without knowing the whys and wherefores of a sacred site, the experience of visiting one can be powerful."

GULF BREEZE
Florida

S ince 1987, Gulf Breeze, Florida, has been the scene of more UFO sightings than any other town in America.

Thousands of witnesses—including police, local government officials, pilots, business people, and teachers—have reported seeing strange objects in the sky. And many of these people have taken startling photos and videos of these UFOs.

There have been so many sightings that people gather nightly at local parks and beaches for what they call "skywatches" in hopes of spotting a UFO. The weekly newspaper *The Islander* even runs a regular column describing the latest sightings.

TV crews from network shows such as *A Current Affair, Encounters,* and *Sightings* have captured the objects on video. Meanwhile, reporters from all over the world have flocked to the tiny town across the bay from Pensacola, Florida, to see for themselves. More often than not, they leave with a good story.

Meanwhile, investigators have documented hundreds of remarkable sightings. The objects have appeared during the day and at night. Sometimes they show up daily; other times, only a few times a month.

"Something truly amazing is going on in the skies over Gulf Breeze," declared Don Ware, regional director of the Mutual UFO Network, an international organization of UFO researchers. Ware said the town has topped all known UFO "hot spots" in terms of the number of sightings and number of years that these objects have been seen.

It all began in November of 1987. Local builder Ed Walters was sitting in his office at home when he noticed a glowing, bluish-gray craft hovering behind a tree.

"This was right out of a Spielberg movie that had somehow escaped from the film studio," Walters recalled in his book *The Gulf Breeze Sightings*. "It was impossible, but there it was, glowing and gliding along like a cloud. There was a quiet in the air. As I stared at the craft, the hairs on my arms bristled. This was no movie prop gone astray."

His first thought was to call the police, but he knew no one would believe him without proof. So he grabbed an old Polaroid camera—which took instant pictures—and ran outside to snap photos.

"My brain was numb," he recalled. "I was out-and-out stupefied. This was a UFO. The camera in my hand almost slipped from my grip. All my attention focused on the bright glow of the power source radiating energy unlike any earthly craft."

He said the UFO was about two hundred feet (61 m) above the ground, moving silently without disturbing any trees. The saucer-shaped object had a dome on top with large dark squares and diamonds around its main body, which he assumed were windows. In between these squares were what looked like portholes. Underneath the craft, in its center, a light that seemed to be a power source throbbed with energy.

Stunned beyond belief, Walters began taking pictures when suddenly the UFO sent down a beam of blue light that nearly paralyzed him. "I couldn't even move my eyes or eyelids," he recalled. "I thought that I was dying. I was trying to breathe. There was air, but my chest wouldn't expand."

About twenty seconds later, he said, his feet lifted off the ground, and he heard a deep, computerlike voice in his head say, "We will not harm you." When Walters screamed, the strange voice ordered, "Calm down." By now, Walters was about four feet (1.2 m) off the ground. The frightened, helpless man then smelled a sickening odor as if ammonia had been mixed with cinnamon. The smell stung his lungs. And then a weird hum filled his head. Suddenly he fell to the pavement, and when he looked up, the UFO had disappeared.

Walters wondered if he was crazy. With shaky hands, he gathered up the photos he had taken and went back inside and looked at the fairly clear pictures of the UFO. "There it was, on the film," he recalled. "It hadn't been my imagination, or some sort of hallucination. What I had seen was real. That wasn't a comforting thought."

He told his wife, Frances, who had arrived home moments after the incident, about his fantastic encounter. "She just didn't want it to be true," he said. "The idea that extraterrestrials not only existed but went around picking up people was something neither of us wanted to admit. But the evidence was right there with us. The photographs and the smell that still clung to my clothes couldn't be explained away."

Wondering whether other people had seen the same UFO, Walters sent the photos to the local newspaper, which published them on the front page. Within days, more than a dozen witnesses called the newspaper to say that they too had seen a UFO.

Over the next three months, residents continued to report new UFO sightings. Walters claimed that he not only photographed the same UFO several times but was actually harassed by aliens. They weren't evil, he said, just rude, because they would occasionally paralyze him and then communicate with him through telepathy. They said things like, "We have come for you," and "Do not resist us," and "Photographs are not permitted."

Once, he claimed, the aliens actually confronted him right outside his house. He said they were about four feet (1.2 m) tall and wore silver spacesuits when they showed up on his patio, waving weapons that looked like cosmic cattle prods.

It sounds like a bad movie, but Walters swears it's real life—and he says he can prove it. He has about forty photos of UFOs that he shot over the months during which the aliens supposedly pestered him, usually in the middle of the night. (Unfortunately, there are no photos of the aliens in his collection.)

The photos have undergone extensive study by a variety of experts. Although no one can say for certain that the pictures are genuine, there has been no proof that they have been doctored.

In fact, Walters's story and his photos underwent an intensive investigation by the Mutual UFO Network. The MUFON report concluded that "the evidence and the accumulated testimony of Ed Walters for his UFO experiences are still valid." In other words, they think he's telling the truth.

Despite those who refuse to believe his story, thousands more do. That's because they have seen with their own eyes UFOs zipping, darting, and hovering over Gulf Breeze ever since Walters revealed his startling account.

One particular type of UFO has been spotted so many times that the locals have a name for it—Bubba. Skywatchers describe Bubba as a dark, disk-shaped object that has a bright red power ring. The UFO turns from a brilliant red to a bright white before it simply vanishes.

Bubba apparently isn't shy. In 1992 it put on a show for thousands of residents who had gathered along the bay for the

Fourth of July fireworks show. Shortly before the show, Bubba appeared and hovered for eight minutes over Pensacola Bay while amazed people pointed and cheered. When the fireworks started, the UFO continued to hover at an altitude of about 8,000 feet (2,400 m). That was thousands of feet higher than any of the fireworks or the several private planes that were circling over the bay.

A few months earlier, a film crew for the TV show *A Current Affair* was shooting video of a local skywatch of forty people when Bubba showed up. The UFO changed color several times. At one point, it glowed bright white before turning back to ruby red. Producer Lila McMurry said she could see a ring of lights on the bottom of the UFO as it passed overhead. The video revealed the object had eight separate points of light.

For the first several years, Bubba usually followed a pattern, averaging an appearance about every third night. Occasionally it would show up on three or more nights in a row—the record is eleven straight. Most often it was seen between sunset and two hours later. But since 1993 it has shown up less frequently, replaced by other kinds of UFOs. In most cases, the UFOs hover silently, then glow extremely bright before zooming off at incredible speeds.

A man who was fishing with his wife provided *The Islander* newspaper with a common description of a typical Gulf Breeze UFO:

"Suddenly, the whole area around us lit up bright as day. Looking upward in amazement, we both saw an enormous white light which remained motionless and soundless. It almost seemed like we could touch it. . . . We felt no heat.

"For several seconds it quietly [lit] the ground around us. We could not see any person behind the white glow of the light. We had an uncanny feeling that somebody or something

75

was intently watching us. I don't know how long we stayed there as we stared spellbound and speechless.

"In an instant the light, in a tremendous burst of speed, started to [rise]. There was no sound, and the air did not stir. The light traveled straight up at a fantastic speed to a point high in the northern sky where without a split second pause it made an abrupt square turn." He said the UFO followed a flight path like a giant figure seven before it vanished.

A group of UFO investigators known as the Gulf Breeze Research Team conducted a sixteen-month probe. They studied over two hours of videos taken during 130 UFO sightings and scores of photographs shot by witnesses.

"Consistently, we have ruled out airplanes and helicopters," said Patti Weatherford, a spokesperson for the group. She said unlike UFOs, airplanes can't hover and helicopters can't hover without making a sound. "Also, helicopters and airplanes cannot suddenly radiate brilliant flashes of light and then simply disappear without a trace."

Members of the research team once tried to communicate with a UFO. It happened during a skywatch in March of 1992, when at least thirty witnesses watched five UFOs darting around in the night sky for ten minutes.

"The UFOs didn't fly in, they just kind of 'blinked in' from nowhere," said witness George Crumbley, a visitor from Baton Rouge, Louisiana. "There were so many at one time that it looked like the sky was blooming with them."

As an experiment, the research team aimed a powerful spotlight at the closest UFO and flashed a series of signals. According to team member Art Hufford, the UFO responded to their signals by repeating their series of flashes. Then the UFO moved closer to them before it suddenly disappeared.

Investigators discovered that at least one UFO left behind a strong magnetic field.

A resident, who asked that her name be withheld, was pulling into her driveway around six-thirty P.M. when she saw a circular craft rising rapidly from behind her home. The bottom of this metallic object seemed to glow. As the UFO rose, it flipped onto its back and then vanished.

The next morning, investigators examined her property. They noticed a pond behind the woman's house had been disturbed. Using a device called a magnetometer, they discovered an unusually strong magnetic field in a small cluster of pine trees behind the house. Readings made two days later at the same location showed the strong magnetic field was no longer there.

Some people in Gulf Breeze claim they have been slightly injured by a UFO.

In 1993 a resident who asked to be called only by the first name Bill told *The Islander* a bizarre story.

While he was on the eastern end of Pensacola Beach at sundown, he spotted a UFO. Suddenly his face felt hot and then extremely cold. He sat on the ground, feeling nauseated and faint.

About a minute later he recovered, stood up, and looked for the UFO. It was gone. After gathering his composure, he went home, where he noticed a small amount of blood on the back of his right hand. At first he thought he must have hit it on something. But when he cleaned it up, he was shocked. The wound consisted of a circle of seven separate and evenly spaced punctures with another puncture in the center. (The newspaper ran a photo of his injured hand.)

Bill soon learned that at least three other persons had similar wounds after seeing a UFO.

"Bill showed me his hand and said he was a little concerned about it because it hadn't healed, only gotten worse," wrote reporter Bland Pugh, who is also MUFON assistant state director. "When he first discovered the marks, they were only small [punctures], now they [were] progressively getting larger. . . . When Bill talked to the doctor, Bill was told that [the doctor] had seen this type of wound before."

Over the years, residents have captured UFOs clearly on video and on film during daylight sightings.

In 1993 resident Martin Allen saw what he thought was a UFO streak across the afternoon sky. Hoping to catch it on video tape, he set up a camcorder on his sundeck and pointed it in the direction that the UFO was last seen.

"I couldn't believe my eyes when I first saw that round silver thing racing across the sky," recalled Allen. "When it shot overhead a second time, I knew it wasn't a normal airplane. It was round and kind of crown-shaped with a lower level and a dark red circle in the bottom center."

Five days later he filmed the UFO a second time as it hovered over the water before it zoomed out of sight. "It was fast, real fast," he said. "I couldn't believe this was happening and that it was happening in broad daylight."

The videotapes were examined by professional photo analyst Jeff Sainio. He said that the object could have been speeding at several thousand miles an hour.

"The second tape shows the UFO accelerated, slowed twenty percent, then surpassed two thousand miles [3,225 km] an hour, all in under one-tenth of a second," said Sainio. "The overall shape of the object resembles, but is not identical to, the shape of objects photographed by Ed Walters in 1987 and 1988." Walters's photos were published later in his book.

Although the Gulf Breeze UFOs often fly over a navy air station and an air force base, military officials deny they know anything about the objects.

However, in 1994 Walters took a series of photos that

78

seems to show that an air force base in nearby Pensacola sent three F-15 fighter jets to intercept a UFO.

Walters said he was looking out the window of his waterfront home one morning when he saw a UFO hovering over the Gulf Breeze peninsula. He grabbed a 35-mm camera with a telephoto lens and ran outside.

As he began to take his first shot, he saw a fighter jet heading for the UFO while two other jets flew above the object. He snapped photos as the jet streaked by the UFO and made a wide looping turn. After the two other jets joined up with the first, they headed for the UFO. As they came closer, the UFO zoomed away. But Walters had it all on film.

"One picture absolutely was phenomenal," said Bland Pugh. "The jet aircraft was covering about a quarter of the UFO, which was in the background. [The pilot] had rolled the aircraft to the right so that he could get a better look as he passed the UFO.

"The picture clearly shows . . . a UFO that looks like a vertical football with rounded ends and a ring of balls or spheres around its center line."

After analyzing the photos, expert Jeff Sainio stated, "These photos are amazing, some of the strongest evidence I have ever seen in my twenty years of photo analysis. I say to you with absolute confidence that there is no evidence of trickery."

He concluded that the F-15 fighter was about 1.6 miles (2.5 km) away from Walters at the time the photos were taken. Sainio calculated the width of the UFO at thirty-two feet (9.75 m) and estimated that it was five hundred to one thousand feet (150 m to 300 m) away from the jet.

Declared government physicist and UFO researcher Dr. Bruce Maccabee: "These photographs prove two things. UFOs are real—and the military knows it!"

Walters said he turned the photos over to experts to further prove the existence of the Gulf Breeze UFOs. "To this day, the naysayers keep trying to say that all the hundreds of UFO witnesses in Gulf Breeze are crazy," said Walters. "And naturally the official statement from the military is 'no comment.'"

So why would UFOs choose Gulf Breeze to conduct their aerial acrobatics? UFO researcher Kenneth Lloyd Larson believes he has an answer.

On a map showing the Earth spread out flat, Larson drew a circle covering the farthest tips of North and South America. The circle touched the extreme northwest edge of Alaska and the extreme southern tip of Argentina. Guess where the center of this large circle is? None other than Gulf Breeze, Florida!

"I've concluded that the UFOs came to Gulf Breeze because they knew that the site represented the center of North and South America," Larson explained.

Meanwhile, the skies over Gulf Breeze continue to light up with UFOs. "Over the past several years, the Gulf Breeze and Pensacola Beach area has been swamped with UFO sightings," said MUFON official Gary Watson. "All I can say is, keep looking up!"

BROWN MOUNTAIN GHOST LIGHTS VIEWING AREA

Brown Mountain, North Carolina

"Look, above the ridge line!" shouted the young woman. The half dozen people who had gathered at a nearby overlook turned their gaze to where she was pointing.

"There it is!" a teenage boy yelled.

"There's another one!" said a third onlooker.

"It's so spooky," said the young woman. "I've got the chills."

Members of the small gathering were staring at a sight that has baffled eyewitnesses for centuries—the Brown Mountain Ghost Lights.

On this particular night, the people saw four pale white lights that turned yellow and seemed to have faint halos around them. The lights moved up and down over the 2,600-foot (793-m) high mountain in the foothills of the Blue Ridge Mountains in western North Carolina. The ghost lights, looking twice the size and brightness of a large star, seemed to skip along the top of the ridge. They wiggled and wavered in the darkness for several minutes before fading away.

"That was so cool," said one of the witnesses, a thirteen-year-old boy. "They're so eerie. Now I know why they call them ghost lights. They're creepy and, well, ghostly."

From the earliest times, the lights have appeared around Brown Mountain. They usually move up and down and can be seen only from a distance. They tend to vanish as you try to get closer to them.

Usually visible when the moon isn't bright or is hidden by clouds, the Brown Mountain Ghost Lights are colorful globes that rise in the sky over northern Burke County about one hundred miles (160 km) northwest of Charlotte, North Carolina. Sometimes witnesses see only one light. But often on dark nights, the lights pop up so thick and fast it's nearly impossible to count them all. They range in color from yellow to light blue to blood red.

The lights can be seen up to fifteen miles (24 km) away. At some points closer to Brown Mountain, the lights resemble zooming balls of fire from a Roman candle. Sometimes they rise to various heights and then fade slowly. Others expand as they rise, then burst high in the air like an explosion, but without making a sound.

Every scientific attempt to explain the appearance of the ghostly Brown Mountain Lights has failed. They have attracted the attention of numerous scientists and historians since German engineer Gerard William de Brahm recorded the mysterious lights in 1771.

De Brahm said that Brown Mountain gave off a gas that was carried by the wind. When a breeze from the opposite side bumped into the wind, it caused the gas to glow like bright balls before petering out. Today's experts don't believe that theory.

The U.S. Geological Survey conducted an investigation in 1913. It claimed that the lights were reflections from lanterns of wagons and headlights of locomotives in the Catawba Valley, south of Brown Mountain. However, the explanation was disproved three years later in 1916 when a great flood swept through the valley, washing out railroad bridges and roads. It took weeks before the roads and bridges were repaired.

During the time when the trains and wagons were blocked

from rolling through the valley, the ghost lights continued to appear as usual.

In 1919 researchers from the Smithsonian Institution and the United States Weather Bureau came to Brown Mountain to study the ghost lights. Bureau official Dr. W. J. Humphries announced that the lights were an unexplained weather phenomenon. But few people believed him.

Years later a second U.S. Geological Survey came up with a different conclusion. It said the ghost lights were due to the spontaneous combustion of marsh gases. But there were no—and still aren't—marshy places on or near Brown Mountain.

The official report also ruled out the possibility that the lights were coming from mountain moonshine stills (structures in which homemade liquor was brewed over fires).

Other scientists concluded that the lights came from glowing rocks. But in 1940 researcher Hobart Whitman analyzed rocks and soil from Brown Mountain and the surrounding area for any unusual elements. The rocks and soil didn't differ from those across the entire western region of North Carolina.

More recently, some scientists announced that the lights are a mirage. Through a peculiar atmospheric condition, they say, the glowing balls are reflections of light from the town of Lenoir, thirty miles (48 km) away. But these same scientists admit that their theory has a big hole in it—the lights were clearly seen long before electricity was invented or, for that matter, long before the town even existed.

To this day, many people of all faiths, ages, and educational background believe the only real answer is that the lights are the ghosts of those who have died on Brown Mountain.

"It's the only explanation that makes sense," said local researcher Ian Bell. "Ghost lights are usually in the shape of balls or irregular patches of light that defy natural explanation. That's what these are—and they've been seen here for centuries."

Rosemary Ellen Guiley, executive vice-president of the International Society for the Study of Ghosts and Apparitions, has written about ghost lights. They often vary in size and shape. "They may be active for years," she said. "Some appear and become 'inactive' after short periods of time.

"Ghost lights have the power to fascinate, and some individuals who see them do not want the mystique spoiled" by an unproven scientific explanation, she said.

The Ghost Research Society, based in Oak Lawn, Illinois, collects data on ghost lights and has identified five common characteristics:

• They appear in remote areas.

• They are elusive and can be seen only from certain angles and distances.

• They react to noise and light by moving away or disappearing.

• They are often accompanied by humming or buzzing.

• They are often associated with a haunting due to a terrible accident or tragedy that took place at the site.

According to Ian Bell, those traits all describe the Brown Mountain Ghost Lights. "The more we learn about the history of this region, the more convinced we become that these are indeed the lights of ghosts who are destined to march forever back and forth across the mountain," he said. "It all started with the Cherokee."

Cherokee Indians were familiar with these lights as far back as the thirteenth century. According to Native American lore, the Cherokee and Catawba Indians fought a fierce battle back then near Brown Mountain. A generation after the battle, the mysterious lights began to appear. The Cherokee believed the lights were the spirits of Indian maidens who went searching for the spirits of their husbands, brothers, fathers, and sweethearts who had died in the battle.

The belief was passed down to early frontiersmen, who soon noticed that when friends or loved ones died a tragic death in the area, strange new lights would appear on Brown Mountain. According to one account in the early 1800s, a young man was supposed to run away with his sweetheart in the middle of the night to get married. But on his way, a flash flood from a fierce storm swept him to his death. When he failed to appear, his girlfriend died of a broken heart. Days later, when a glowing light began hovering around Brown Mountain, family and friends became convinced that her spirit was still waiting with a lantern in her hand for her boyfriend's arrival.

In another account a few years later, a beautiful girl was torn between two boyfriends. She finally chose one. When his rival learned she had given her heart to the other man, the rival murdered him. The girl eventually became sick and died. A mysterious light soon appeared, causing people who knew her to believe that her spirit was carrying a candle and searching for her beloved.

Even more people became believers in the ghost lights in the mid-1800s after learning of the terrible saga of a married couple, Jim and Belinda, who lived deep in the woods of Brown Mountain.

Jim had a terrible temper, and neighbors often saw Belinda with bruises on her. One day, Belinda disappeared. When family and friends questioned Jim, he said his wife had put on her bonnet, left the house, and never returned.

Because no one believed him, a search began for the young woman. Two miles (3.2 km) from the cabin, a relative of Belinda's found her bonnet. It was stained with dried blood. As searchers concentrated their efforts in the wooded area where the bonnet was found, a fire unexplainably broke out and destroyed any further evidence of Belinda's whereabouts or of any foul play. Many people suspected Jim started the fire on purpose.

The blood-stained bonnet was not enough evidence to convince authorities that Jim had murdered his wife. Family and friends of the missing woman felt helpless and disappointed. There was nothing more they could do.

But then a bizarre new glowing ball of light that kept changing color began to appear on Brown Mountain. Night after night they watched in fascination, knowing the eerie light held some special meaning. One evening, two elderly women followed the light. Carrying oil-burning lanterns, they walked through undergrowth until they were directly under the bright glowing ball. There, they found a pile of stones at the bottom of a high cliff. They unpiled the stones and discovered the skull of a grown person.

According to a mountain myth, the skull of a murder victim never decays. It remains intact for a reason. When the skull is held aloft over the head of the killer, he or she cannot tell a lie about the crime.

The skull was taken to Jim's cabin right away. Two strong men restrained Jim in his chair while a third man held the skull over Jim's head. Then they asked Jim if he had killed his wife.

He turned pale and began to tremble, afraid to say a single word in his defense. It's not clear what happened to him. Some said he went insane; others claimed he suffered a strange illness and died. Most believe that he was hanged.

In 1913 the *Charlotte Daily Observer* reported that three fishermen were spooked by a ghost light. "The mysterious light is seen just above the horizon almost every night. . . .

With punctual regularity it rises in the southeasterly direction just over the lower slope of Brown Mountain. It looks much like a [fiery] balloon, a distinct ball . . . and very red." Supposedly, the light appeared after the death of one of the fishermen's friends.

According to a 1925 account, an "observer who was standing about eight miles [12.8 km] from Brown Mountain says that suddenly after sunset there blazed into the sky above the mountain a steady glowing ball of light. To him, the light appeared yellowish, and it lasted about half a minute, when it disappeared rather abruptly. It appeared to him like a star from a bursting skyrocket, but much brighter."

Not everyone, of course, believed the strange lights were spirits from the beyond. Many lumberjacks in the area assumed the mysterious colored lights were caused by the reflection of lanterns off rare gems lying on the mountain's face. For years, lumberjacks searched in the darkness for gems clear and powerful enough to reflect light from the moon. Unfortunately, they never found such gems.

To this day the Brown Mountain Ghost Lights continue to make their eerie appearances. One of the best spots to see them is Wiseman's View, located on a United States Forest Service road at Linville Falls. Another good vantage point is at a turnout called Lost Cove Cliffs, at mile marker 310 on the Blue Ridge Parkway. At an elevation of 3,805 feet (1,160 m), the turnout offers a view of Brown Mountain and, if you're lucky, the bizarre lights—whatever they might be.

"In recent years, scientists have been more concerned about exploring outer space," said North Carolina author Nancy Roberts, who writes about ghosts in the region. "Perhaps they have forgotten that there are mysteries on our own planet still unsolved. The Brown Mountain lights are one of them."

HANNAH HOUSE
Indianapolis, Indiana

E ver since Hannah House was used to help slaves escape from the south to the north in the years before the Civil War, it has become one of the most haunted places in America.

Residents and visitors to the historic redbrick mansion, located on Madison Avenue in Indianapolis, Indiana, have experienced many unexplained phenomena. People have seen ghostly figures wander the hallways, smelled the sickening odor of death, and heard crashing glassware that is never found.

"So many things go on there," said parapsychologist Ruth Loux. "Doors that have been locked suddenly open and slam closed by themselves, cold drafts are felt when no windows are open, sounds of footsteps are heard on the stairs, and spoons have been seen lifting from cups and flying through the air."

Dale Kaczmarek, who heads the Ghost Research Society, said that after visiting Hannah House he considered it one of the top ten most-haunted houses in America.

The stately but spooky twenty-four-room mansion was built in the 1850s by Alexander Moore Hannah. A well-known and admired man, Hannah was an Indiana state legislator, postmaster, sheriff, and clerk of the circuit court.

Prior to the start of the Civil War, Hannah—a man of conscience—made it known he was against slavery. He allowed his home to be used as a station of the Underground Railroad—a series of safe houses where runaway slaves could stay during their escape from the south to Canada.

Because people who helped escaped slaves in those days faced prison if caught, homeowners were very careful. Hannah hid the slaves in his basement during the day. Late at night, he and his servants would load the slaves into a horse-drawn wagon, cover them up with a tarp, and quietly transport them to the next house along the Underground Railroad.

One night someone accidentally knocked over a lantern in the basement, causing a deadly fire. Several slaves were trapped in the flames and died. The fire damaged both the basement and other parts of the house. Later, when the mansion was repaired, the original basement was covered over.

Psychics and paranormal investigators believe that the spirits of the fire victims have been haunting the house.

Ruth Loux visited Hannah House with a psychic several times, trying to find the cause of the bizarre phenomena, especially the awful odor.

"We had no difficulty agreeing that we experienced a 'feeling' about one particular room," she told Richard Winer, author of *More Haunted Houses*. "After being in the room about fifteen minutes, we heard noises—eerie sounds of moaning and whining, and soon a heavy, sickening odor was detectable. My companion on the investigation complained of a headache, and I became nauseous. It was a smell of flesh, of death, and we went outside for fresh air.

"Upon returning, our hostess took us to the basement, which was free of the dampness usually found in basements. It was here, our guide said, that the slaves had hidden. We made five trips to Hannah House in a period of one year, and each time the sounds and odors in the one room and the basement never changed."

Librarian Nadine Moore told the *Indianapolis Star* that she felt scared after visiting the basement.

"Something was there, standing beside me . . . an awful presence that could be sensed but not seen," she said. "As soon as I walked down into the basement at Hannah House, I could feel it. I left the basement when the vibrations intensified and became uncomfortably strong."

Gladys O'Brien and her husband John were bothered by strange, unexplained smells, sounds, and sights. From 1968 to 1978, the couple ran an antique business in the house and sometimes lived there as well.

"There's a bedroom upstairs that has a very strong smell of rotten flesh," she said. "I'd be working in that room for a short time, and up from the floor would come a terrible smell that would come and go. I scrubbed that floor with carbolic acid and we even painted it. But the smell persisted, so we just closed the door and used the room for storage. But we had to keep that door closed all the time anyway. Otherwise, we had disturbances out in the hall—doors opening and closing by themselves, strange noises, that sort of thing."

John said that the odor would change from sickening to sweet in a room where the door opened and closed by itself. "I walked in there one morning, and it smelled like something or someone had been dead for a long time," he said. "I tested the floor to see if something had crawled under the boards and died, but I never found a thing. The next instant, the whole atmosphere changed, and the room smelled just like a rose garden. I thought maybe there was something wrong with my sense of smell, but my wife also noticed the odor, and so did other people who visited and didn't know a thing about the house."

Spirits of slaves aren't the only ones that may inhabit

Hannah House. The O'Briens and visitors have seen or felt the presence of many other ghosts.

"It didn't take me long to figure out that we had other inhabitants in the house—unseen ones, that is," John O'Brien told Winer. "Every time I'd go into the upstairs rooms, I could tell that something was with me. I could feel it, but I couldn't see a thing.

"The house seemed to feel hostile toward my wife and me. We supposed it was because it had been vacant for six years. Vandals had broken in during that time, and we figured that was why the ghostly occupants were stirred up.

"But other unexplainable things kept occurring. I came in one evening and walked across the floor. I took about three steps, and each time my foot touched the floor it sounded like somebody was underneath, banging the floorboards with a sledgehammer. That happened many times. My wife experienced it too.

"Sometimes when we were watching TV upstairs, I'd hear footsteps loud and clear. When I turned down the set and walked downstairs to the first floor, I could still hear those sounds. And the stairs were carpeted too. We couldn't hear our own footsteps, but each one of the spirits made different sounds; some would go thump, thump, thump. Then you'd hear light footsteps and clothes rustling. But the noises would stop when I'd get all the way to the bottom of the stairs."

John claimed he saw the ghost of an elderly man staring at him from the stairs. "I could see right through him," he said. "Before I could say 'boo,' he turned and headed for the hallway. I jumped up off the sofa to follow him, but he just disappeared. It was definitely a [spirit] or a ghost; it wasn't solid flesh or anything like that. You could actually see through it."

John said the ghostly man was dressed all in black,

wearing clothes from the nineteenth century. He had muttonchop sideburns and a medium build.

One time, Mrs. O'Brien escorted two psychics who were investigating the Hannah House hauntings when she encountered a ghost. Recalled Mrs. O'Brien, "While they were here, I was in the room where the odor is. In my mind's eye I saw a very elegant-looking old man and heard him say, 'Get downstairs and take care of your own business and leave these fool women alone!'"

One evening the O'Briens' son was alone painting a room in the mansion when he had an uneasy feeling that someone was watching him, recalled Mrs. O'Brien. The next night he brought his family over for company. His youngest daughter said she saw a strange elderly man in a rocking chair on the first floor. The man rose from the chair and began walking up the stairs before disappearing. A search of the house revealed that, other than the family, no one else was there.

The O'Briens' son was painting the room because the professional painter who had been hired to do the job became spooked by the spirits. "The house rejected him," said Mrs. O'Brien. "Pictures fell off the walls and doors closed by themselves when he was around.

"One day I served him some coffee in the old nursery. I poured the coffee and put the spoon back down on the tray, turned away for a second, and glanced back just in time to see the spoon fly off the tray and hit the wall—all by itself. I tried to convince the painter that it had been caused by the vibrations of a passing truck, but that didn't work. He quit."

For years people have heard loud crashes of glass in the house, but they've never found anything broken.

Current owner David Elder recalled an incident that happened when the house was unoccupied. "It had been empty for years. I was downstairs in the main part of the house when there was a loud sound of glass breaking. It seemed to come from the basement. I thought maybe someone had broken in and had knocked over a barrel of fruit jars. But when I ran downstairs, no one was there."

Mrs. O'Brien said she heard the sound of crashing glass at least five times. "One time two deputy sheriffs were called in, and they both heard the noise."

Her husband, who also heard the crash several times, said it sounded like a china cabinet falling down. "You could hear glass break and wood crunch," he said. "You could look all over the house but you wouldn't find anything that tipped over or fell. It didn't happen at regular times, but in the middle of the night or early in the morning."

Over time, the spirits eventually seemed to accept the O'Briens, he said. "We could almost see it changing. Instead of the house feeling hostile, it seemed to become friendly. We could actually sense it.

"I can trace it back to one Saturday night when I was watching TV on the second floor. There was no light on in the hallway. Then suddenly I heard this [terrible] sound, and it wasn't coming from the TV set. So I turned the sound off and opened the door to the hall. There was definitely someone or something groaning out there. Then it stopped, so I went back to watching TV again. But about an hour later, it started all over again. So I said out loud, 'If I can help you, please tell me. If I can't, then go somewhere else to do your bellyaching.' And the groaning stopped."

Mrs. O'Brien said the ghosts upset her for a long time until she got up the nerve to talk to them. "Finally, I said, 'Look, we're protecting the house, and you're scaring me.' After that, they didn't bother me too often."

After the O'Briens left Hannah House, the ghosts continued to make their presence known—especially around

Halloween, according to Beth Scott and Michael Norman, authors of *Haunted Heartland*.

From 1980 to 1982 the Indianapolis Jaycees used the mansion for their annual "Haunted House" project. They rigged up fun, eerie effects for the people who would walk through the creepy place. But some of the spookiest effects weren't created by the sponsors—or any other person.

In 1980 owner David Elder and project coordinator Dick Raasch were relaxing with fellow workers in the kitchen. Suddenly, their conversation was interrupted by bizarre scratching sounds coming from inside the landing wall of an old stairway used years ago by servants. Elder ducked beneath the stairs but failed to find the source of the noise.

Days later, the spirits apparently fiddled with the stereo that Raasch had installed to play the chilling sound effects for the Halloween tour. Raasch and a friend were alone in the house listening to the stereo when it unexpectedly turned off. Raasch and his friend checked the stereo and found that someone had pushed the On/Off button. They turned it back on. Later, the stereo stopped again. No one else was in the house—and all the doors and windows were locked.

"Someone pushed that button," Raasch claimed. "But there was no way someone else could have been inside the house."

The following year a TV crew from a local station visited Hannah House to shoot a segment for Halloween. They wound up with more than they bargained for.

One of the cameramen stood in the dining room doorway in order to take a shot across the room. Pointing to an old chandelier that hung from the ceiling, he asked the crew, "Wouldn't it be eerie if the chandelier moved?" At that instant the chandelier started to swing on its own.

"Our mouths were open [in amazement]," recalled

Raasch, who, along with six other people, witnessed the chandelier sway by itself. There was no one upstairs who could have jumped on the floor to set the chandelier in motion. All the doors and windows were closed and locked, so no breeze caused it to move. And no hidden wires led to the chandelier.

On that same day, the TV crew followed psychic Allene Cunningham as she walked through the mansion. She sensed "cold spots," telltale areas that suggest the presence of ghosts.

In a room known for spirit activity, the cameraman was shooting the TV program's host, who was standing in front of a coffin that had been placed against a wall. Suddenly, a picture above the coffin fell to the floor. The nail was still on the wall. Not only that but the wire on the old picture remained firmly attached to the frame.

"There is no conceivable way the picture could have fallen of its own accord," said Raasch. "It lifted up and fell. It just looked like somebody dropped it on the floor.

"I can't explain the incidents. Something was in [the house], but I just don't know what it was."

Psychics and ghost hunters continue to investigate the mansion, but have yet to find all the answers to the Hannah House hauntings.